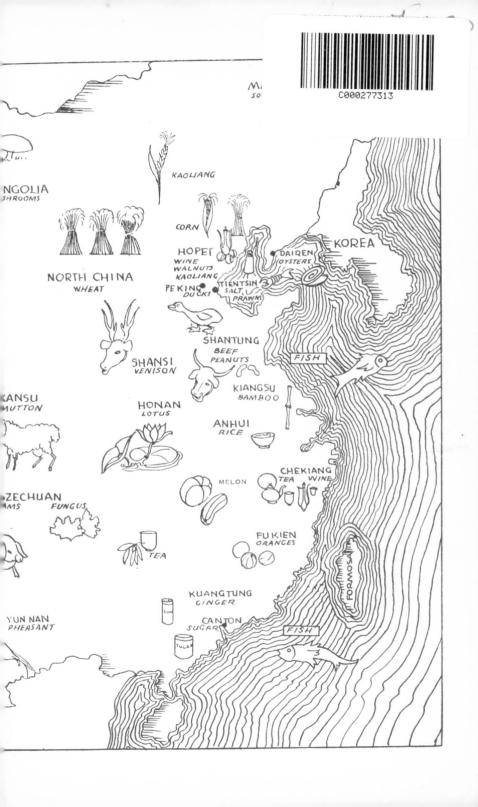

M...
SO...

NGOLIA
SHROOMS

KAOLIANG

CORN

HOPEI
WINE
WALNUTS
KAOLIANG

NORTH CHINA
WHEAT

PEKING
DUCKS

TIENTSIN
SALT
PRAWNS

DAIREN
OYSTERS

KOREA

SHANSI
VENISON

SHANTUNG
BEEF
PEANUTS

FISH

KANSU
MUTTON

HONAN
LOTUS

KIANGSU
BAMBOO

ANHUI
RICE

ZECHUAN
MS
FUNGUS

MELON

CHEKIANG
TEA   WINE

TEA

FUKIEN
ORANGES

FORMOSA

YUN NAN
PHEASANT

KUANGTUNG
GINGER

CANTON
SUGAR

GIN

SUGAR

FISH

THE CHINESE FESTIVE BOARD

Chafing Dish

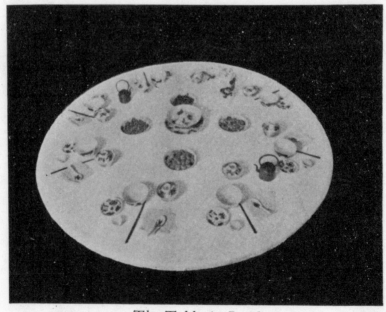

The Table is Laid

THE CHINESE FESTIVE BOARD

Corrinne Lamb

HONG KONG OXFORD
OXFORD UNIVERSITY PRESS
1985

Oxford University Press

Oxford New York Toronto
Petaling Jaya Singapore Hong Kong Tokyo
Delhi Bombay Calcutta Madras Karachi
Nairobi Dar es Salaam Cape Town
Melbourne Auckland

and associated companies in
Beirut Berlin Ibadan Nicosia

© Corrinne Lamb 1935

First published by Henri Vetch, Shanghai, 1935
This edition reprinted, by arrangement with Kelly and
Walsh Limited, in Oxford Paperbacks 1985

ISBN 0 19 583956 0

OXFORD is a trade mark of Oxford University Press

Printed in Hong Kong by Ko's Arts Printing Co.
Published by Oxford University Press, Warwick House, Hong Kong

INTRODUCTION

IN no other country does the matter of eating present such serious problems as in China. For the masses it represents a daily struggle against overwhelming odds to obtain food enough to keep body and soul together. To those Chinese, on the other hand, who are more fortunately situated, eating takes on a serious aspect in a different sense. With them it is an affair involving pleasant anticipation, careful thought, meticulous selection, and, finally, a wholehearted if somewhat noisy gusto during the process itself.

Over a period of twenty years it has been my pleasure to partake frequently of Chinese hospitality, not only in the gay Treaty Ports, but more often in the distant reaches of China's vast interior. The honors have been equally divided between princes, governors, generals, peasants, inn-keepers and yea, camelteers. In this way I have learned that Chinese cooks possess that rare ability to work the same marvels with the lowly cabbage purchased for a string of cash that they do with birds'-nests at sixteen dollars an ounce.

Happy memories of mine hosts are inseparably linked to lingering thoughts of their abundant hospitality and the delicious food which graced their tables. With the object of making at least some of these dishes available to others I have compiled this little book. The several chapters on the amenities of eating I have introduced in order that the uninitiated may learn some of the conventionalities of the Chinese festive board. I hope that the strangers to this land may find them interesting; to the foreign guests within its borders may they succeed in being both enlightening and helpful.

To Messrs. H. J. Timperley and Henri Vetch I owe a debt of gratitude for their generous assistance in my work, as well as their constant encouragement.

The Proverbs which precede the chapters of this book have been taken from various sources, particularly from *A Collection of Chinese Proverbs*, by Scarborough and Allan.

CORRINNE LAMB.

Peiping. August 1934.

CONTENTS

PART ONE

ILLUSTRATIONS

PROVERBS

When you put on your clothes, remember the weaver's labor; when you take your daily food, remember the husbandman's hard work.

身披一縷常思織女之勞
日食三餐每念農夫之苦

Feed moderately on wholesome food; garden herbs surpass rich viands.

飲食約而精園蔬逾珍饈

With three good meals a day be content; take in your sail after a good run before the wind.

飽餐三飯常知足得一帆風便可收

Talk to those who understand, and give food to those who are hungry.

說話說與知音送飯送與饑人

A man won't pine on three meals a day, or go in rags if he has three suits.

飯有三餐不餓衣有三件不破

CHAPTER I

Dinner is Served

IT would be well perhaps if we first altered some of our preconceived notions regarding the Chinese diet. Many people think that the Chinese live entirely on rice; some believe that rats also occupy an important place on the daily menu. Both ideas are mistaken and should be discarded. Rice does form a staple in the diet of approximately two-fifths of the Chinese people, but the majority of the five hundred millions depend upon wheat, barley and *kaoliang*, the last mentioned being a sort of Chinese millet. As for rats—such things are never heard of, though it is true that snakes are eaten in South China.

With the Chinese coolie, eating is a precarious business. Gnawing hunger supplants the dinner gong, and the destitute seek food wherever it may be found at the time. The peasant, the shop-keeper, the artisan, the small manufacturer—these and certain others abide by a more regular schedule. Two meals a day is their lot, with a *petit déjeuner* shortly after rising, if so inclined.

In countries where the *petit déjeuner* is favored it is usually a very slight meal indeed and falls far short of a British or American breakfast. China is no exception to this rule. A cup of tea, accompanied by a ring of light batter fried in deep fat, is the universally accepted thing in Cathay, and I warn you, you would not like it. It is a sort of prehistoric doughnut. Cold, limp, insipid, and shining in its coat of cooled grease, it is not at all the sort of thing which would appeal to one at seven o'clock in the morning. We can safely and speedily pass over this business of a Chinese breakfast. It leaves much to be desired.

At about 10 a.m., however, the thoughts of the nation turn to food. Much work has already been done, the appetite has become keen, and for a long time already the restaurants and teashops have been bestirring themselves in the interests of supply and demand. With people of the lower classes the main and most substantial part of this first meal is a basis of either rice or flour. The rice is invariably steamed, and even in the humblest Chinese home it is better by far than the sticky, glutinous mess which is prepared so poorly abroad.

Flour is prepared in many forms. There are neat little round cakes, baked to a brown in a mud oven; pale woe-begone little doughballs, which have been steamed over a huge boiling pot in a mesh basket woven from split bamboo; huge cart-wheels of *man t'ou* or native bread, baked and cut in slices; *mien t'iao erh* (spaghetti); *yu ping* (oil cakes), round biscuits fried in deep sesame oil; *pao tzu* (steamed rolls with a filling of ground meat and vegetable); and occasionally some sweet condiment.

These are the important members of the family. There are also cousins, aunts and uncles and even little step-children, but these can be ignored. Rice and flour are the basis of the meal. With the better class Chinese from one to four dishes are usually served with the staples. These are called *ch'ao t'sai* (炒 菜) and it is here that the Chinese chef shows wonderful versatility.

You can *ch'ao* practically anything from a marsh shrimp to a buffalo steak, providing you have the proper imagination. The essentials to the accomplishment of this feat are threefold : oil, soya sauce and vegetables. Needless to say there are certain combinations which have become standardized and have endured throughout the centuries. Thus, one may take a very small quantity of minced mutton, cabbage cut fine, oil, soya sauce, give a twist of the wrist and—*voilà!* Or, a very small quantity of minced pork, small celery shoots cut fine, oil, soya sauce and again—*voilà!* Occasionally a mushroom or two conceals itself in the mixture, or a bit of ginger-root cut very fine. There are myriads of combinations and the chef is governed by what he finds available in the market. Only the better class Chinese find it financially possible to acquire vegetables, fruits and edibles not in season.

To many hundreds of thousands even one *ch'ao t'sai* is denied and some simple alternative is resorted to. This may be a bowl of noodles, meagerly covered with a hot red-pepper sauce, or a bowl of rice with a few minced salt turnips. Such simple additions relieve the monotony of rice or flour eaten alone and give a bit of zest to the simplest meal.

The better class Chinese are more self-indulgent. Perhaps one can illustrate the point better by giving a simple menu for the average family residing at home :

MENU

炒 韭 菜
ch'ao chou t'sai
(sautéd leeks and pork)

炸 丸 子
cha wan tzu
(fried meat balls)

榨菜湯
cha t'sai t'ang
(thin vegetable soup)

炒扁豆
ch'ao pien tou
(sautéd string-beans and pork)

炒木鬚肉
ch'ao mu hsü jou
(eggs and mushrooms)

花捲合大米飯
hua chuan ho ta mi fan
(wheat bread with or without rice)

The evening meal is taken between four-thirty and six o'clock. In all cases this is slightly more elaborate than the morning repast, but this probably is governed to a very great extent by the state of the purse.

An element of great importance and one which has a great bearing on this engaging matter of eating in China is the widespread habit of nibbling at food between the regular meals. Throughout the day everyone indulges in titbits of food according to his fancy in the matter. Fruits, candies, cakes, nuts, and biscuits are offered for sale by itinerant vendors and small shops. Every railway train, theater, teashop, bath-house and bazaar has its allurements for those feeling the first twinges of appetite. From this has resulted a pronounced irregularity in meal hours, consistent with the irregularity characterizing most other Chinese activities.

PROVERBS

In dress and food do not break rules.

穿衣吃飯不犯條律

If you rattle your chopsticks against the bowl, you and your descendants will always be poor.

敲碗敲筷窮死萬代

Better slight a guest than starve him.

寧可慢客不可餓客

Hurry men at work, not at meat.

催工莫催食

CHAPTER II
Table Etiquette

ALTHOUGH it is undeniably true that there are certain advantages in the niceties and refinements of Western table manners, still, many of our conventions, carried out in their most rigid form, do not permit of a full enjoyment of food. Whoever has freely gnawed his chicken bone, buried his face in a slice of juicy watermelon, or dipped his bread in the gravy will know exactly what this means.

The Chinese have developed a multitude of conventions which are concerned with the matter of eating. But few of them govern the actual consumption of food, and the diner in China feels almost complete liberty to indulge as he thinks best. *Sui pien!* ' Suit yourself ' is the golden rule of eating.

In the first instance, the service of food involves none of the complications of foreign table etiquette. What we know as chopsticks are really called in China *k'uai tzu*, which, in turn, may be freely translated as "quick little boys." This term is applied to them on account of their nimbleness and speed when once in action and it is a most appropriate name. One pair of *k'uai tzu* constitutes the entire cutlery equipment per person, unless by some chance a small porcelain spoon is available or called for to contend with a soup or other thin liquid. One bowl per person completes the table service. Many weary American housewives might well wish that their dishwashing worries could be reduced to such

a minimum. Table linen there is none, thus
eliminating another unnecessary item.

Nearly all Chinese food, when served, has been
previously sliced, carved, minced or reduced in
some manner to proportions which need no further
dissection, and when once placed upon the table
it is fair prey to all present. Let us assume that
four or five hot *ch'ao t'sai* have been placed upon
the table, each diner having been served a bowl
of rice beforehand. There is no awkward hesita-
tion and no waiting. Life is serious and food is
life. There ensues a simultaneous dive of chopsticks into the various dishes, the diners suiting
their own fancy as to what they desire to concen-
trate upon after liberal sampling of the various
offerings. Food is never passed. A certain priori-
ty is accorded the elders for the first few moments
but after that it is a matter of every man for himself
and the devil take the hindmost. As all the food
is served in one course, there is ample opportunity
to gauge one's capacity. One is never left to
wonder whether there may not soon appear some
delicious unknown dish which must be passed
up with regret due to previous over-indulgence.
There is no element of mystery in a Chinese meal.

Tea is served immediately before the meal and
immediately after. No napkins are provided but
several times during the meal a servant will enter
with an adequate number of small rough towels
which have been wrung out in boiling water. Each
diner accepts one, wipes his face and hands, and,
thus refreshed, settles back to his task with new
vigor and enthusiasm. Of all Chinese customs I
know none so luxurious as this, and my undying

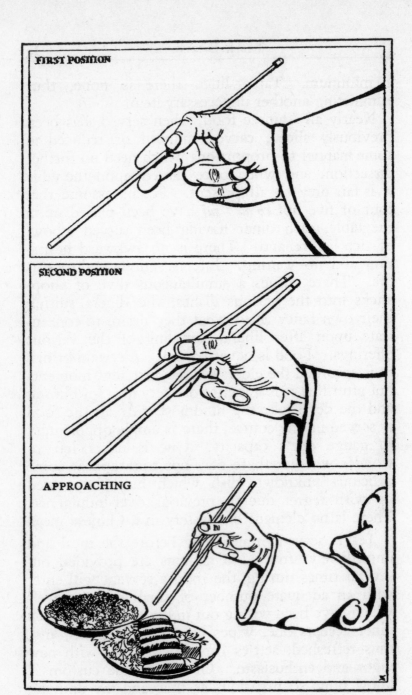

FIRST POSITION

SECOND POSITION

APPROACHING

PICKING UP FLAT PIECES OF FOOD

PICKING UP BITS OF FOOD

PICKING UP APPLES
Illustrating the capabilities of Chopsticks.

thanks will go to the first American hostess who puts her dainty Irish linen serviette carefully back in the linen chest and serves me occasionally with a steaming Turkish towel.

The Chinese dinner table is also not subject to the awkward conventions of late arrivals and early departures. One does not have to get a permit from his host to retrieve the missing kerchief. One arises and departs with a firm step and an unblushing countenance, returning with equal confidence and continuing the noble work which he has started. When one has eaten his fill he departs immediately. A bowl of tepid water with which to rinse the mouth is customarily offered and for this purpose one seeks the garden, an open window, or any number of handy receptacles which are there for the purpose. There is no occasion for after dinner speeches, humorous stories, hard peppermint candies or any of the other devices which the European has invented to detain the parting guest. It was purely a matter of food, and there being no further need for food, the event has reached its conclusion.

Domestic pets also enjoy this freedom and it is rare indeed that the cat or dog will not be found secreted beneath the table at the beginning of a meal. The discarded chicken bone finds its proper haven on the floor, but not for long. It is a simple but effective way of cleaning up.

PROVERBS

Receive all guests that come, making no difference between relatives and strangers.

客無親殊來者當受

He who keeps the hills, burns the wood; he who keeps the streams drinks the water.

管山的燒柴管河的吃水

In ordinary life you must be economical; when you invite guests you must be lavish in hospitality.

居家不可不儉請客不可不豐

He who cannot in his own house entertain a guest, when abroad will find few to entertain him.

在家不會迎賓客出外方知少主人

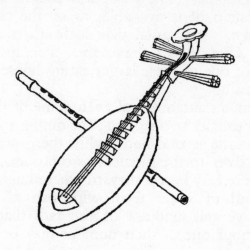

CHAPTER III

A Chinese Dinner Party

L ET us now consider that much heralded event, a Chinese dinner party. The American or European invites his guests to dinner; in China the invitation is issued to EAT (*ch'ing ch'ih fan*) and here lies the precise difference.

Needless to say there are formal and informal dinner parties. The distinction lies in certain rites and ceremonies rather than in dress, table etiquette or food. The host may well bid by word of mouth a few friends to dine with him, and, if so, the informality of the affair will be understood. On the other hand invitations, written on huge oblong sheets of red paper, might be circulated. It would then be known that the affair was to a degree formal.

Rare indeed is the banquet which is held within a private home. The exception occurs when no fitting restaurant is available, as in the case of a small town. It is usual that such affairs are held in a *fan kuan tzu* or restaurant. Perhaps a brief glimpse of one of these larger eating houses would be interesting.

Modern restaurants, and even some of the older ones, are usually two-storied; the dining rooms are located on the second floor, while the ground floor is given over to the kitchens, storerooms, offices, etc. There may be a courtyard where huge earthen crocks full of water teem with fish of various kinds, alive and ignorant of the fact that within the half-hour one of their number may be gracing the banquet board. The manager and his staff of clerks hover close by the doorway, eager to welcome the guest and fulfil his wishes. Behind, ranged along their battery of clay stoves, stand the chefs—each one is a specialist in his own class of food.

"Hai-sheng", that short, fat little fellow, prepares only fish and would not touch a chicken on a bet. "Sun-fu", the long, lanky gentleman with a face like a pirate, concentrates on ducks. He despises "Hai-sheng", for after all anyone can cook a fish. But a duck—ah, there is a difference!

Practically all restaurants cater both *à la carte* (點菜, *tien tsai*) and *table d'hôte* (整桌, *cheng cho*), the latter by prearrangement. The following are two typical examples :

A LA CARTE

花熘里几
hua liu li chi
(fried fresh pork)

熘丸子
liu wan tzu
(meat balls)

爆肚領
pao tu ling
(sheep stomach)

熘肥腸
liu fei ch'ang
(sliced sausage)

里几絲拌粉皮
li chi ssu pan fên p'i
(pork with bean curd)

鷄絲拌洋粉
chi ssu pan yang fên
(chicken with bean curd)

燴三鮮
hui san hsien
(stewed tripe)

木鬚湯
mu hsü t'ang
(soup with eggs)

花捲
hua chuan
(steamed bread)

大米飯
ta mi fan
(rice)

高湯臥果
kao t'ang wo kuo
(thin soup with poached eggs
to moisten the rice with)

A TABLE D'HÔTE MENU

(The dishes are listed in the order in which they are served)

Leng Hun 冷葷 HORS D'OEUVRES

桃 仁
t'ao jên
(almonds)

杏 仁
hsing jên
(apricot kernels)

瓜 子
kua tzu
(watermelon seeds)

松 子
sung tzu
(pine-nuts)

香 蕉
hsiang chiao
(bananas)

橙 子
ch'ên tzu
(oranges)

蘋 果
p'in kuo
(apples)

鴨 梨
ya li
(pears)

火 腿
huo t'ui
(sliced ham)

燻 魚
hsün yü
(smoked fish)

海 蜇
hai chê
(seaweed)

素 鷄
su chi
(sliced chicken)

Ch'ao T'sai 炒菜 ENTRÉES

熘 小 鷄
liu hsiao chi
(stewed chicken)

燴 蝦 仁
hui hsia jên
(stewed shrimps)

熘 魚 片
liu yü p'ien
(fish fillets)

燴 海 參
hui hai shên
(stewed bêche-de-mer)

Cheng Shih 蒸食 STEAMED DISHES

黄 糕
huang kao
(cakes)

蜂 糕
fêng kao
(honey cakes)

蒸 餅
chêng ping
(steamed rolls)

飽 子
pao tzu
(steamed dumplings)

Ta T'sai 大菜 MAIN DISHES

燕 窩
yen wo
(bird's-nest soup)

魚 翅
yü ch'ih
(shark fins)

魚 肚
yü tu
(fish stomachs)

鮑 魚
pao yü
(abalones)

銀 耳
yin erh
(tree fungus)

鴿 蛋
kê tan
(pigeon eggs)

K'ao Hsiao 烤 燒 ROASTS

燒 鴨
hsiao ya
(roast duck)

烤 小 猪
k'ao hsiao chu
(roast suckling pig)

Fan Shih 飯 食 RICE DISHES

八 寶 飯
pa pao fan
(rice pudding)

大 米 飯
ta mi fan
(rice)

湯 麵 餃
t'ang mien chiao
(meat dumplings)

大 米 粥
ta mi chou
(congee)

叙

馬連良謹訂

席設崇文門外豆腐巷七號

五月二十三日星期四下午一時潔樽候

TRANSLATION

(Reading from top to bottom, and from right to left)

The fifth month, the twenty-third day (*Thursday*), *one o'clock in the afternoon* "*chieh tsun hou*" (*a conventional phrase in Chinese meaning* "*the cups will be cleaned and your presence awaited*").

(*Mr.*) *Ma Lien-liang respectfully writes:*

"*The feast is arranged*" *outside of the Hatamen Gate, Bean Curd Lane, No. 7.*

Let us assume that Mr. Lan Yu-chin, a gentleman of culture and learning who derives his monthly stipend from a government connection, has thought of giving a little dinner party to seven of his friends. Mr. Lan has specified four-thirty p.m. at the "Bright Illustrious Springtime" Restaurant. The management is all aquiver. It is five o'clock, yet no Mr. Lan. True, Mr. Wang and Mr. Chu have called and inquired, but on learning that Mr. Lan had not arrived they left word that they would go to take a bath and return later. No one is in the least upset. And now Mr. Lan arrives, busily clanging the footbell of his rickshaw. He descends and enters. The manager takes a deep breath, leans well back, lets out one lusty shout: "Lan Hsien-sheng!"; and faces peer over the rickety balustrade to catch a first glimpse of the patron of the evening.

Barely has Mr. Lan been led to the room which he has engaged than there comes another lusty yell from below. Messrs. Wang and Chu have returned. Good! The others? Oh, they will come. It is only five-thirty. By six they are all present, and there now ensues that exciting business of seating the assembled guests. The accompanying diagram depicts the proper arrangement and recognition of each diner's importance; unfortunately the plan does not reveal the commendable modesty and the loud protestations of the guests themselves. In assigning places to his friends the Chinese host is guided by their official and social status, but the one predominating factor is age and the associated reverence for one's elders.

In actual practice a host endeavouring to seat his guests according to the best ethics of the game resorts to devices ranging all the way from polite suasion to something closely approaching physical violence. The guest, on the other hand, is at liberty to air his protest of unworthiness of such honor, but usually subsides and rests contentedly in his assigned seat after sufficient coercion.

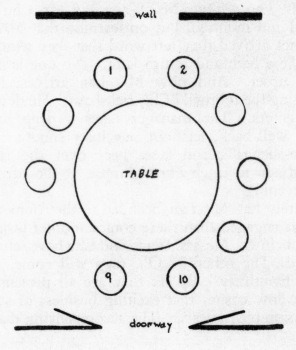

Beginning with Seat No. 1 guests are arranged in the order of their importance. Seats 1 and 2 are for guests of honor. Seats 9 and 10 for the hosts.

Immediately after Mr. Lan and his friends have settled down into their places around the huge circular table covered with a length of cotton sheeting which days of continual use have now turned a dull grey, tea is served, also peanuts and watermelon and pumpkin seeds. It requires the skill of a parrot to open the seeds, but centuries of practice have enabled the Chinese to accomplish this between their front teeth. The generally accepted practice it to swallow the kernel, and to blow the shells to leeward.

"And what to eat?" says Mr. Lan, our host.

The waiting servant has placed in front of him a sheet of paper, a brush pen and a slab of ink. Each guest makes one or several selections. Mr. Lan frequently protests that there will not be enough to eat and urges them to make another choice. As a final gesture of true hospitality he adds two or three dishes of his own preference and the order is now handed to the servant.

Then things begin to happen. Poised at the stairway the waiter bellows at the top of his voice the written order. As each item is made known to the company of cooks below, there is a shout of understanding, a frantic grab for a pot or kettle and a mad dash into the storeroom.

Wine is served. Perhaps it is *huang chiu*, not unlike sherry. For ambitious folks it will be *pai ka erh* or *hsiao chiu* an innocent looking beverage, white in color, which augurs sudden death. For the fastidious *mei kuei lu*, a rose-scented wine with a habit of sliding down gracefully and politely, and smacking you ten minutes later for your trouble. *Hors-d'œuvres* make their appearance. Sliced ham, cold chicken vinaigrette, ducks' tongues with mustard sauce, "Ming Dynasty" eggs*, delicious candied walnuts.

These are the drinking dishes. Now begins the clever but noisy game of *hua ch'uan* (matching fingers for drinks). Mr. Wang has lost six times in succession, which means that he has been compelled to consume a like number of drinks, and his face is beginning to look like the setting sun. Mr. Ch'ien, on the other hand, is a man with a drinking reputation who has not lost once, and therefore all of his libations have been purely voluntary. Mr. Ch'ien is beginning to feel that for him the party is a waste of time. Mr. Lan is making strenuous efforts to keep things going. He suggests a *kan pei* (bottoms up), and everyone drains his little cup in one gulp. The party is getting properly under way. Mr. Wang now feels inclined to sing, so he sings. Conversation is becoming more difficult, but what does it matter? Mr. Wang wants to sing. Good. Let him sing.

The first dish has arrived. There is a sudden silence. Mr. Wang stops singing just as Mr. Lan poises his chopsticks above the huge vessel in the center of the table. It is the conventional sign to dive in. There is a loud sound as of escaping steam. The dinner is on.

---

*"Ming Dynasty Eggs" is a fictititious name given to eggs best prepared in South China. Duck eggs encased in a coating of mud, wheat chaff and tea are subjected to fireside roasting for four or five hours. The resultant chemical and physical changes have led foreigners to believe that such eggs had been buried many year—which is not true.

Mr. Lan has thought that perhaps some of his guests are bored. Perhaps they wish some novel distraction! Some dainty little acquaintance in a nearby sing-song house to lean on and whisper sweet nothings to. Splendid! The messages are despatched. The ladies arrive, all a-twitter and furnishing olfactory evidence of their acquaintance with the cheapest brand of Japanese scent. One of them will now sing. A lusty shout brings her violinist, body-guard, cashier, and general factotum —all in one. She sings. The violin screeches. Mr. Liu maintains a steady pressure on the sharks' fin soup under the very nose of the singer but it does not bother her in the least. Only if Mr. Liu's soup actually became entangled in the violin would she be concerned. The Chinese are like that.

With the appearance of the bowls of rice, all drinking has stopped. The ladies have hastened away to attend other nearby parties. The eating has become more laborious until finally it stops altogether. Hot towels arrive for the last time. Everyone arises and seeks his hat. Gastric noises among the guests are accepted by Mr. Lan as proof of his hospitality. A few words of thanks are offered. Mr. Lan conceals in his hand the account rendered for twenty-six courses of food. Smiling upon his guests he remarks with every appearance of conviction and sincerity :

"I dare not stand before you ; there has been nothing to eat!"

PROVERBS

Earth has no feasts which do not break up.

天下無不散的筵席

Friends while good dinners last; husband and wife while fuel and food remain.

酒肉朋友柴米夫妻

Whilst travelling don't reckon the distance; whilst eating don't reckon the quantity.

行不計路食不計數

The mouth is an unlimited measure.

口是無量斗

CHAPTER IV

The Life of the Party

THE Chinese are most temperate in the matter
of drinking intoxicating beverages. Indeed a Chinese who imbibed at other than
meal times or who would take strong drink without
the accompaniment of food would be a curiosity.
At the same time there are those who do not drink
at all, others who partake in modest quantities, and
lastly, a fraternity of staunch souls who have developed a real capacity and set a fast pace at the festive
board.

To enliven the dinner party the Chinese have
invented a number of games which are played by
two or more guests and in which the reward or
penalty, whichever it may be, takes the form of
indulgence in the flowing bowl. One which has
survived the greatest number of years and which
still reigns supreme is known as *hua ch'uan* (樺 拳),
the matching of fingers. The Italians have a similar
game, but unquestionably the Chinese were the
original patentees and are past masters in the game,
which requires an agile hand as well as an alert
mind.

Let us briefly describe *hua ch'uan* in its simplest
form. First of all a guest may challenge a
fellow diner to play. It must be understood that
the playing of fingers is only permissible during
the "drinking courses" of the meal and usually
ceases when the more substantial food makes its
appearance. Mr. Wang having challenged Mr. Wu
to match fingers, both guests are immediately
provided with a cup of spirits, wine or brandy.

(In recent years brandy and beer have both found greater favor with the Chinese, but the native products still hold their own and are preferred by the vast majority.) Wu accepts Wang's challenge and faces his opponent. The right hand of each contestant is then raised and the forearms are simultaneously advanced. At a mutual signal the forearm is retracted, again quickly thrown forward and either a closed fist or any number of fingers are extended. At the same time each player loudly shouts his estimate of the total number of fingers shown on both hands. To guess the correct number and to deceive one's opponent is the object of the game.

For example, let us assume that Wang has challenged Wu and they are now ready to play. Rapidly both players' forearms are retracted and extended, Wang extending three fingers and shouting "six", while Wu has extended one finger and shouted "four". Wu is the winner and Wang is compelled to pay the penalty of drinking his cup of wine. The cup is immediately refilled and the game is resumed until an agreed number of cups have been drained or the play terminated by mutual consent. Of course, there are many occasions when the guesses of both players are wrong and in this event the forearms are quickly retracted and extended again. Among expert players the arms and fingers are moved in perfect synchronization and any hesitancy or attempt to deliberately cheat or deceive an opponent calls forth a penalty.

. The Chinese have developed a great many combinations of words and numbers which not only serve to announce their estimate of the total number of fingers but which also provide a sing-song rhythm which controls the tempo of the game. Below is given one of the commonest codes employed :

Closed fist (no fingers protruding)

	(對　手)	*Tui shou*
1 finger	(一　品)	*I p'ing*
2 fingers	(兩榜第)	*Liang pang ti*
3 fingers	(三星照)	*San hsing chao*
4 fingers	(四　喜)	*Ssu hsi*
5 fingers	(五　魁)	*Wu k'uei*
6 fingers	(六　順)	*Liu shun*
7 fingers	(七　巧)	*Ch'i ch'iao*
8 fingers	(八匹馬)	*Pa p'i ma*
9 fingers	(快發財)	*K'uai fa t'sai*
10 fingers	(全福壽)	*Ch'uan fu shou*

If knowing how to play *hua ch'uan* is important, then knowing how NOT to play the game is equally essential. There are "don'ts" which one should carefully remember. In putting forth one finger, never extend the index finger as this is a form of insult which is certain to be resented by a Chinese. In extending two fingers employ the thumb and index finger; never the index and middle finger as this is a gesture which will also be resented.

The various elaborations of this merry game are too many to set forth in detail in such a small volume as this, though the version of it known as *k'ai i ko tang p'u* (開 一 個 當 舖) or "opening a pawnshop", should not escape honorable mention. Two *chang kuei ti's* (掌 櫃 的) or managers, are

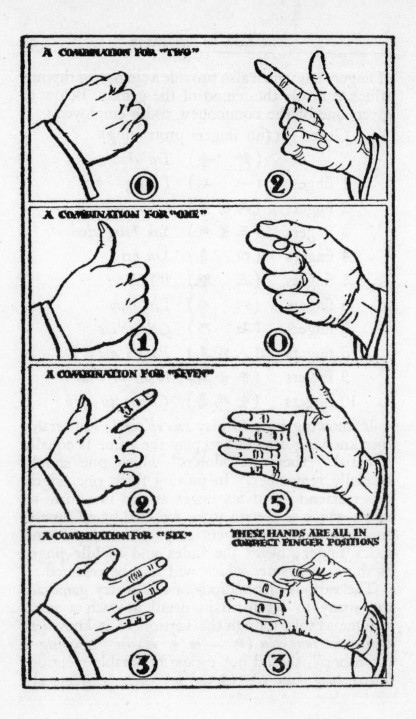

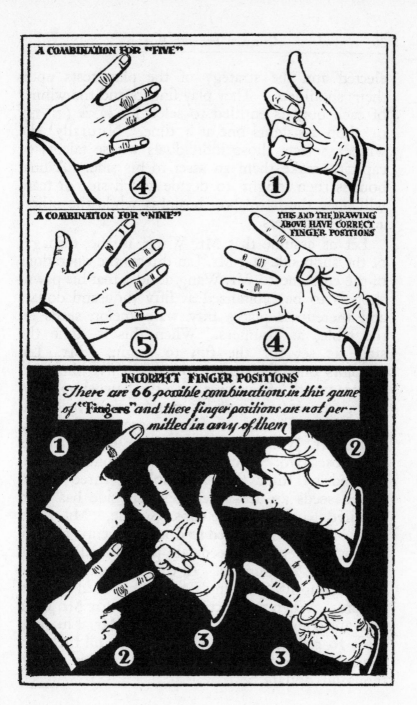

elected and the strategy of the play rests upon their shoulders. They play fingers and the winner of each bout is entitled to select his *ho chi* (夥 計), or shop assistants one at a time. Naturally, the winner selects those individuals whose talents or capacity make them an asset to his side. A final bout is then fought to decide which side or team will open the pawnshop business while the others act as customers.

Let us assume that Mr. Wang is the manager of the shop side and Mr. Liu directs the operations of the customers. Mr. Wang decides that his pawn-shop is to be capitalized at fifty thousand dollars and thereupon places fifty water-melon seeds on the table, as counters. When this is done the stage is set for the fun to begin. Mr. Liu appoints one of his party to transact five thousand dollars worth of business with the pawnshop. Mr. Wang appoints one of his clerks to act in behalf of the firm. Five bouts of fingers are played, during which Mr. Wang's side loses three and Mr. Liu's party loses two. Thus, Mr. Wang's capital has been reduced by three thousand dollars, three water-melon seeds are discarded, and his side has been required to drink three cups of wine, Mr. Liu's party has been compelled to drink two cups of wine and two watermelon seeds are placed on their side of the table as counters. In this manner the game proceeds until Mr. Wang's capital has been reduced to zero. When this occurs, the tallies for Mr. Liu's side are counted up. If it has cost Mr. Liu sixty seeds to reduce Mr. Wang's capital to nil then Mr. Wang's business has shown a net profit of ten thousand dollars.

Another game which is always sure to enliven the festivities has been adopted from the Japanese game of *Janken pan* (ジヤン拳). The method of play somewhat resembles the Chinese game of *hua ch'uan*, but is much simpler for the uninitiated. We may call the game "stone, scissors and paper" because these are the three symbols which control the play. An outstretched palm represents a sheet of paper, a clenched fist represents a stone, and the index and middle fingers extended represent a pair of scissors. The hands of two opponents are simultaneously thrown forward. Thus Mr. Wang extends scissors and Mr. Wu extends a stone. As the stone will dull the scissors Wu wins the bout. Again, Wang extends paper and Wu extends a stone. As paper can wrap up the stone Wang becomes the winner. Again, Wang extends paper and Wu extends scissors. As the scissors can cut the paper Wu wins again in this case. In the event of two scissors, two stones, or two papers being displayed the bout is a draw and play is resumed.

Another aid to hearty drinking, and one which is sure to produce a large toll of victims is the "match game". No brains whatever are required for this. A safety match is ignited and clamped upright in the sliding cover of the box. The box is then passed from right to left, from one guest to another, the idea being to keep it alight as long as possible. Intentional delay in passing, blowing the match out and shaking the box are not permissible. Whoever holds the box when the last glow disappears has the dubious privilege of draining his cup. As matches burn but a very short while you are at liberty to make your own estimate of the dangerous features of this sport.

Last, but not least, is the famous Chinese game of
"Twenty-one". And if this sounds too simple or
childish to demand your serious attention then permit me to suggest that you try it. You will marvel
at the deficiencies of your primary education. Elect
some member of your party to start to count with
"one". The counting proceeds clockwise. When
the count has reached seven, seventeen, twenty-
seven, thirty-seven, etc., that person whose count
it is must remain silent and merely tap the surface
of the table. When the count reaches fourteen,
twenty-one, twenty-eight, thirty-five, or any mul-
tiple of seven beyond that, that person whose count
it is must remain silent and tap the bottom of the
table. The unfortunate mathematician who mis-
counts pays the penalty. I repeat, if you think
this is simple, just try it!

For those enticed by the lure of out-and-out
gambling perhaps the nest of wine cups which
modern Chinese have had bequeathed to them
from their forefathers will add charm to the festive
board. Beginning with a porcelain or ivory cup
the size of a thimble, each fitting snugly within the
shiny bosom of his next of kin, such a set terminates
with a cup the size of a teabowl, the draining of which
is fraught with vast possibilities. Folded paper
slips bearing numbers corresponding to those ap-
pearing on the face of the wine cups are drawn
by the diners, and the fortunate and the unfortunate
are required to pay the penalties which Fortune
decides for them. For instantaneous results this
merry pastime is endorsed by the very best Chinese
undertakers.

PROVERBS

Intoxication is not the wine's fault, but the man's.

酒不醉人人自醉

Every glass of wine and every slice of meat are predestined.

杯酒塊肉皆前定

Good wine reddens the face; riches excite the mind.

好酒紅人面財帛動人心

When you drink from the stream, remember the spring.

飲水思源

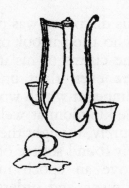

CHAPTER V

The Wine Bowl

PERHAPS the name wine is a misnomer when applied to Chinese intoxicating beverages because in reality they are distillates of rice or *kao liang*, though other cereals are occasionally employed in their manufacture. Concerning their origin it is related that once upon a time, many centuries ago, a chef in the imperial kitchen absent-mindedly overlooked an earthen crock in which he had placed some rice to soak. Several days later he discovered his error and in order to ascertain whether the precious grain had spoiled he quaffed a generous potion of both the rice and the fluid. Almost immediately he was overcome with a highly optimistic outlook toward life and became emancipated from the petty worries and annoyances which had been his daily lot. Although it is not so recorded we can even imagine that he broke into song.

The news of his discovery was prompty reported to the Emperor, who also partook of a liberal sample, and confirmed the claims of his inventive servant. Preparations were even then under way for an enormous state dinner at which would be assembled the nobility of the kingdom as well as envoys from distant lands. Surely, thought the Son of Heaven, to serve this newly found source of mirth and good cheer would prove an epoch in the annals of imperial entertainment, and orders were issued to concoct an adequate supply of this elixir of life.

The Emperor's thoughtfulness in providing for his guests such an unique treat had a tragic sequel to the

Pouring Wine

evening's hospitality. The feast turned out to be an unusually jovial and friendly affair. State dignitaries who formerly were difficult to sway to the Emperor's point of view had agreed without a murmur to his every suggestion. Stiff-necked ministers who ordinarily sat throughout such banquets in dignified silence had become the life of the party. A risqué story even found its way into the evening's proceedings and provoked unrestrained laughter and applause.

It was the custom of China's imperial rulers to hold audience and transact State business at four o'clock in the morning, since men's minds were held to be more alert at that early hour. Hence before dawn on the morning after the banquet the Emperor seated himself upon the Dragon Throne and waited expectantly for his subordinates to present themselves. But, alas, not one of them turned up. Hastily messengers were despatched to investigate, returning one after another with the news that the errant nobles had been rendered oblivious to the charms of early rising—so much so that no amount of shaking or threatening had any effect upon them whatsoever.

The Emperor thereupon occupied himself with formulating a set of rules and regulations governing the matter of drinking. First he decreed that the soup bowls which had been used the evening before were taboo, and in their stead small cups holding about two thimblesful should thereafter be used. Thus we learn the origin of the present-day Chinese *chiu pei* or winecup. Secondly, it was commanded that anyone desirous of quaffing the flowing bowl must eat at the same time—not heavily, nor greedily, but sufficiently to provide an absorbent basis for the wine. So, we discover the origin of the Chinese *lêng hun* or hors d'œuvre. Finally, he insisted that while drinking, guests should engage in a mild form of physical and mental exercise; so as to keep them on their feet, or on their seats maybe. The game of *hua ch'uan*, or playing fingers was thereupon invented. Though this trio of bye-laws is not obligatory, in this day and age it may be considered the source of Chinese drinking customs. That it has contributed enormously to the admirable moderation and dignity of Chinese drinking no one can possibly deny.

China, like many European nations, has its connoisseurs of wines. In Chinese eyes, a good wine is one which has been manufactured carefully enough and hoarded a sufficient number of years to make it pleasing to the taste, beautiful in colour and devoid of any traitorous after-effects on the following morning. Forty years is considered a modest age for a really good wine. Naturally, such old vintages may be purchased only by people of means. The cheaper grades are available to the most humble however, and it is greatly to China's credit that though some may be better than others they are all fit for human consumption, while the best grades would delight the palate of the most fastidious foreign judge.

Chinese wines are stored in jars, and are sold by weight, one catty (*chin*) being about one and a third pound. For a dinner for two en tête-à-tête, four ounces (*ssu liang*) is sufficient. Chinese wines are always served hot in little pewter, brass or porcelain pots and are consumed while still warm.

For the guidance of those who wish to test the merits of Chinese wines, or even convince themselves of the wisdom of the Emperor's regulations the following list of the better known wines may be helpful. Prices per *chin* are given in Chinese silver dollars or cents. A Chinese dollar in August 1934 was worth about 33 cents U.S. currency, or 1s. 4d.

CHIU LEI 酒類 CHINESE WINES

Ch'ên Hsiao 陳 紹	A very high class yellow wine, resembling sherry . . . S.$0.64—1.00
Chu Yeh Ch'ing 竹葉青	"Pai kan" flavored and colored with bamboo leaves. . . . . S.$0.64
Fo Shou Chiu 佛手酒	"Pai kan" flavored and colored with pomegranate . . . . S.$0.64
Liang Hsiang Chiu 良鄉酒	A medium grade yellow wine . . . . S.$0.64
Lien Hua Pai 蓮花白	"Pai kan" flavored and colored with the lotus flower (sweet) . . S.$0.64
Mei Kuei Lu 玫瑰露	"Pai kan" flavored and colored with rose petals . . . . S.$0.48
Nü Chên Chiu 女貞酒	Yellow wine of a grade superior to "Ch'en Hsiao". . . . . . . S.$1.00
Pai Kan Chiu 白乾酒	A strong white spirit distilled from corn or "kaoliang" (a type of millet) . . . . S.$0.32
Wu Chia P'i 五加皮	"Pai kan" colored and flavored with various herbs, etc. Considered a medicinal wine. . . . . S.$0.70-0.80
Yin Ch'ên Chiu 茵陳酒	"Pai kan" colored and flavored with artemisia . . . . S.$0.64

PROVERBS

Come, God-of-the-kitchen, whose surname is Chang;
Now here is your pudding, and here is your t'ang,
When you get up to heaven it will make us all glad,
If you tell what is good, and omit what is bad.

灶王爺本姓張有年糕有瓜糖
上天言好事少說是非

With a friend in the cook-house you can get something
to eat; with a friend at court you can obtain office.

廚房有人好吃飯朝中有人好作官

Let there be plenty of food and clothing, and propriety
and righteousness will flourish.

衣食足而後禮義興

Only eat fresh fish and ripened rice.

魚吃新鮮米吃熟

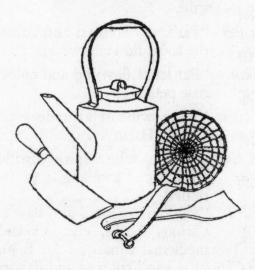

CHAPTER VI

In a Chinese Kitchen

THE following recipes for genuine Chinese food were obtained as the result of actual observation of Chinese cooks (mostly from well known restaurants in Peiping) engaged in the assembling and preparation of each dish. Despite what would appear to be an ideal condition for recording recipes, the difficulties which presented themselves were considerable. The rapidity with which a Chinese chef operates, his disdain for measured quantities, along with his reluctance at times to expose the secrets of his craft, all contributed to the obstacles which had to be overcome before the work was done.

The foreign stove and equipment which were at first provided for what amounted to laboratory tests were eventually discarded in favor of a native mud stove, tin cans, copper ladles, gourds and calabashes. As a result the conclusion was reached that rice can only be cooked in a brass kettle, fish can only be fried in an iron *ch'ien tzu* with a broken handle, mutton can only be stewed properly in a vessel made from an empty petrol can, and tea can only be prepared in a pot with the spout broken off. Dishes should only be washed with a whisk-broom, kitchen utensils should not be washed at all but wiped out, and lusty singing, merry conversation, folk songs and dances should always be engaged in when preparing anything really difficult. And so, gentle reader, the responsibility rests with you. If, boasting an array of bright, glistening enamel ware, you have the latest model electric stove with automatic signals, shut-offs, turn-ons and instrument boards, plus automatic ice-boxes, egg-beaters, dish-washers, and all the paraphernalia of this modern age, you must take the consequences. The following recipes really represent the combined reports of a corps of earnest detectives in a Chinese kitchen. Regardless of what facilities are employed, the recipes are the "real" thing, and the results are bound to be good.

Attention is called first to the all important matter of quantities. The conventional symbols have been employed and when one half-cupful is specified, it is on the understanding that your own judgment will be the final determining factor. Furthermore, it has been realized that certain ingredients may not be available at all times. Thus, when bean flour is called for but is not available, wheat flour would obviously save the day. A canned mushroom might reasonably be expected to perform the same service as a dried mushroom, and so on.

The matter of time also deserves mention. An effort has been made to specify the length of time taken in cooking. Needless to say the degree of heat is the controlling factor in this case and keeping one's eye on the food rather than on the clock will produce infinitely better results.

The name of each dish has been given in three ways. First, in its Romanized form, according to the Wade system, which is the generally accepted method of putting Chinese sounds into written form. Second, an attempt has been made to record the names in a form which can be pronounced by anyone able to read English. And lastly, the

Chinese characters have been appended. The recipes are arranged alphabetically according to the Wade system.

It will be noted that many of the recipes call for *Huang Chiu* (黃 酒), or Chinese wine. Sherry is recommended as a substitute. With the repeal of the Eighteenth Amendment it should not be long before Chinese wine will be available in every major American city, and when that is so its use in preparing Chinese food will be found preferable.

It may be wondered why there are such notable differences in the quantities of ingredients which go to make up the various dishes. Certain of them seem quite ample for six or eight people, while others appear just sufficient for three or four. The reason for this is quite simple. As stated before, the recipes have been recorded while watching Chinese chefs prepare the food under precisely the same conditions as exist in a restaurant. While *cha hsia jên* (炸 蝦 仁), or fried shrimps, is an excellent dish, it would only be served as an entrée during the preparation of a Chinese meal. As such, the quantity is reduced in order to keep it in its proper setting and not to detract from the main dishes which are sure to follow. In the recipes themselves an endeavour has been made in the footnotes to denote the adequacy of each concoction. This, plus a little arithmetic, should enable anyone to multiply or subtract the ingredients according to his own fancy.

PROVERBS

A good breakfast doesn't take the place of a good dinner.

侵晨飯好算不得午後飽

To be careful of clothes is to obtain clothes; to. be careful of food is to obtain food.

惜衣得衣惜食得食

The peony, though large is useless; the date blossom, though small, yields fruit.

牡丹花大空入目棗花雖小結實成

Better return and make a net, than to go down to the stream and merely wish for fishes.

臨淵羨魚不如退而結網

PART TWO

CHAPTER VII

Index to Recipes

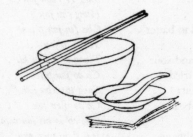

Ingredients of Cha Chiang Mien

CHAPTER VIII

Fifty Selected Recipes

炸炒米肉丸子

1. CHA CH'AO MI JOU WAN TZU

(Pronounced : ja chow me row wan t'z)

(FRIED PORK BALLS)

INGREDIENTS

1½ lbs. fresh pork	1 tsp. sugar
¼ cup soya sauce	1 cup rice flour (米粉)
¼ cup Chinese wine (黃酒)	3 eggs
(or sherry)	1 lb. lard
1 bud garlic	1 tsp. black pepper

DESCRIPTION

This dish consists of small meat balls made from the above ingredients. They are most tasteful and delightfully tender though crisp. Served as the accompanying dish with either rice or "mien" (noodles) they make a splendid luncheon dish.

PREPARATION

With a sharp cleaver and chopping board mince the fresh pork meat. (This is preferrable to putting it through a grinder). The garlic bud should then be finely chopped and added to the meat mixture along with the soya sauce, Chinese wine (or sherry), sugar, rice flour and the whites of three eggs.

Roll between the palms of the hands small balls and fry them to a crisp in the lard which has been brought to the proper temperature for deep frying. Remove, drain and after placing on a serving dish sprinkle with the black pepper.

Approximate time of preparation : 30 minutes
Enough for four people.

炸鷄蛋餃

2. CHA CHI TAN CHIAO

(Pronounced : ja jee dahn jow)

(EGGS, FRIED A LA CHINOISE)

INGREDIENTS

Eggs
½ lb. lard (or sufficient to make melted grease ½ in. deep in
salt and pepper   pan
soya sauce

DESCRIPTION

The following is the Chinese version of a fried egg. It
is well worth a trial.

PREPARATION

Into a frying pan place ½ lb. lard, or sufficient to make
melted lard ½ inch in depth. Break the eggs one by one into
a cup or bowl and pour carefully into the fat—which should
not be too hot. Watch carefully and when a golden brown
turn one half over on the other in the same manner as a
Parker House roll is shaped. Remove immediately from
the pan, place on a sheet of absorbent paper and allow to
drain. When all of the eggs are thus cooked, serve on a
warm platter and sprinkle with salt and pepper.

Soya sauce should be served at the table for those who
wish it.

Approximate time of preparation : 15 min.
Quantity optional.

炸 醬 麵

3. CHA CHIANG MIEN

(Pronounced : ja jeong mien)

(NOODLES, OR MIEN, WITH A THICK,
PIQUANT SAUCE)

INGREDIENTS

½ lb. pork
30 spring onions
1 tsp. chopped ginger-root
½ lb. bean sprouts

½ lb. noodles
1 cup of "chiang" (醬)
4 tsp. olive oil
1 cup water
12 radishes

DESCRIPTION

This is a dish which should particularly appeal to those who are fond of noodles, spaghetti and other flour pastes. In Chinese the word *mien* means flour, but it also means noodles, spaghetti and other forms made from flour, the differences being noted by means of qualifying adjectives. The "chow mien" of the American-Chinese restaurant is really *ch'ao mien* (炒麵), *ch'ao* meaning to fry or fried, and *mien* meaning noodles.

Referring to this particular dish the word *cha* (炸) also means to fry, fried. *Chiang* is the name applied to a particularly aromatic condiment which is made from red kidney beans. It is made best in the Province of Kuangtung, where Canton is located. As it is not subject to decomposition and thus lends itself to export, it is available in Chinese provision stores and can be purchased in any major city.

PREPARATION

Into ½ lb. of pork which has been diced quite small mix four spring onions which have been chopped fine (the green portion should be used as well as the white). Chop the ginger-root very fine until the equivalent of one teaspoonful is obtained. Mix these ingredients thoroughly together. Heat the olive oil in a frying pan and add the above mixture. Fry about five minutes stirring the mixture constantly. Add the cup of "chiang" (醬) while stirring and then add one cup of water, a little at a time, continuing to stir the mixture the while. Cook for about ten minutes.

The remaining onions should be chopped very fine. The radishes should be peeled and sliced lengthwise very thin. The bean sprouts should be immersed in boiling water for about two minutes. These three items are then to be placed on separate dishes and then placed on the dining table.

As the American housewife rarely makes noodles—the manufactured variety having supplanted those home-made—it is suggested that she suit herself as to what type to employ. The short broad variety lends itself better to this dish. The noodles should be prepared in the usual way.

DIRECTIONS FOR SERVING

Serve the noodles in individual bowls. Each person should help himself to the "chiang" (醬) sauce first, placing small portions of the chopped onion, bean sprouts and radishes upon this and mixing them with the noodles.

NOTE

Bean sprouts when canned are not particularly good as they lose their freshness and crispness which is so appetizing. It requires but little effort to sprout a quantity of navy beans which have been soaked in water and placed upon a heavy damp towel or moist earth or blotting paper. The sprouting beans should be kept in semi-darkness, preferably in a cellar.

Approximate time of preparation : 40 min.
Enough for four people.

炸 粉 肉 片
4. CHA FEN JOU P'IEN
(*Pronounced : ja fun row pien*)
(PORK CUTLETS FRIED IN BATTER)

INGREDIENTS

1½ lbs. fresh pork	4 eggs
1 cup Chinese wine (黃酒)	1 tsp. pepper
(or sherry)	1 tsp. salt
1 cup rice flour	2 lbs. lard

DESCRIPTION

Fresh pork fried in batter in deep fat forms the basis of this attractive dish. Indeed it is as good as the main dish of a foreign meal as it is with Chinese food.

PREPARATION

Two hours previous to the actual time of cooking this dish cut the pork into cubes about an inch square. Place the meat in a deep bowl and pour over the Chinese wine (or sherry) to which has been added 1 tsp. salt.

When ready make a batter with the rice flour and the four
eggs which have been briskly beaten, adding a small quantity
of water if too stiff. Bring sufficient lard to the boiling point
and quickly immerse each cube of pork in the batter and
drop into the deep fat. Remove when a golden brown to
a serving dish, sprinkle liberally with pepper and serve.

Approximate time of preparation: 2½ hrs.
Enough for four people.

炸 火 腿 圓

5. CHA HUO T'UI YUAN

(Pronounced : ja haw twae yuan)

(HAM AND EGGS A LA CHINOISE)

INGREDIENTS

1 lb. lean ham
6 eggs
1 tsp. flour

6 slices bread (approximate
2 lbs. lard

DESCRIPTION

It was not left to Europeans and Americans to enjoy a
monopoly of that delightful combination, ham and eggs.
In the Chinese dish "Cha Huo T'ui Yuan" we find a new
version of the union.

PREPARATION

Take 1 lb. of lean, cooked ham, and either put it through
a grinder, or, preferably, mince it very fine with a sharp
cleaver. The six eggs should then be beaten thoroughly
and the ham added. Add sufficient shredded bread (all crust
should have been removed) to make a very thick paste, then
enough flour to enable one to roll the mixture into balls
about the size of a chestnut. Fry in the deep fat until a
golden brown.

Approximate time of preparation: 20 min.
Enough for three people.

炸 蝦 球 兒

6. CHA HSIA CH'IU ERH

(Pronounced : ja shea choa'r)

(FRIED SHRIMP BALLS)

INGREDIENTS

2 lbs. fresh shrimps	4 oz. fat pork
2 eggs	lard

DESCRIPTION

If you care for shrimps at all you will like them even better prepared in this Chinese style.

PREPARATION

After carefully washing, shelling, and re-washing the shrimps the meat should be carefully minced. Add the pork, which has also been minced and mix the two ingredients with two eggs which have previously been beaten until light. Season to taste. Roll into balls the size of a walnut and fry in lard until a golden brown.

Approximate time of preparation: 30 min.
Enough for six people.

炸 熘 黃 菜

7. CHA LIU HUANG T'SAI

(Pronounced : ja leo hwang t'sy)

(THICK SOUP OF EGG, SHRIMP AND HAM.

INGREDIENTS

6 eggs	½ cup Chinese wine (黃酒)
½ cup cooked shrimps	(or sherry)
½ cup diced ham	1 cup chicken broth, or stock
½ cup bamboo shoots (竹笋)	1 tsp. cornstarch
¾ cup lard	½ tsp. salt

DESCRIPTION

The preparation of "Cha Liu Huang T'sai" demands very careful attention as the secret of its making lies in the mixture not being permitted to become lumpy, the finished product more resembling a rich or creamy soup. Only quick action will guarantee this result. This dish may be served either with rice or "mien" (noodles).

PREPARATION

With a pair of chopsticks (or a fork) mix thoroughly together the eggs, chicken broth (or stock), cornstarch, salt, Chinese wine (or sherry). Put the lard in a frying pan and place over a medium fire. Add the above ingredients, increase the heat, and stir the mixture constantly. When the mixture has assumed a creamy consistency quickly add the shrimps, diced ham and bamboo shoots.

Approximate time of preparation: 15 min.
Enough for four people.

炸　碎

8. CHA SUI

(*Pronounced : ja suay*)

(CHOP SUEY)

INGREDIENTS

1 lb. beef, pork, or chicken	1 tsp. sherry
10 mushrooms	1 tsp. sugar
1 onion	2 tsp. lard
1 lb. bamboo shoots	3 tsp. soya sauce
1 stalk celery	

DESCRIPTION

So many stories have been told about the world-famous dish "Chop suey" that it is difficult to place belief in many of them. In point of fact the dish "Chop suey" is unknown in China. "Chop suey" is the Cantonese expression of *Cha sui*, which in the Pekingese colloquial means "fried miscellaneous." This at least gives us some clue to the nomenclature of "Chop suey."

As to the origin of the dish there are many stories. It is said that when the illustrious Chinese Ambassador Li Hung-chang visited the United States he implored his body-servant to prepare him some Chinese food, being utterly wearied of the rich foreign dishes he had been having for many months. Unable to procure the necessary Chinese vegetables, condiments and other essentials, the servant did the best he could and concocted a sort of pot-pourri à la chinoise which was destined to be the grandfather of "Chop suey."

It matters little whether the yarn is true or not. In 1923 a ship-chandler and restaurant keeper known to the foreign community of Shanghai as "Eddy", and dearly beloved by all, decided that the time was ripe for Shanghai to have a modern Chinese restaurant. "Eddy" had long seen eager-eyed tourists clamber down the gang-plank and urge the waiting rickshaw coolies to speed them to some place where they could find "real" chop suey. The pot of gold surely rested at the end of the rainbow and "Eddy's" enthusiasm soon resulted in a very handsome restaurant on Whangpoo Road, complete with electric signs and the essential Chinese insignia for its identification. Then came the dawn. Like Diogenes "Eddy" set forth to find the cook to cook "chop suey" but was met with doubtful looks and evasive answers. It began to look like an overwhelming defeat. But "Eddy" was not the type to succumb to such discouragement. Digging deeper into his purse, he sent an emissary to San Francisco and in due course his deputy returned with a son of China who was making his debut in his native land. With an understanding look and a smiling face the newcomer entered the restaurant kitchen and produced "chop suey."

PREPARATION

With a sharp, heavy knife cut all of the ingredients very, very fine and put to one side. Take a saucepan, put in the lard and bring it to the point where it is very hot. Add the meat. Cook one minute, stirring constantly. Pour in the sherry and soya sauce and cook another three minutes.

In another saucepan place 1 tsp. lard, heat as before and add the mushrooms, celery, onion and bamboo shoots. When these are cooking well add the contents of saucepan No. 1 and cook a further three minutes. If water is required add a little.

Approximate time of preparation : ¾ hr.
Enough for four people.

9. CH'A
(*Pronounced chah*)
(T E A)

INGREDIENTS

"Ch'a yeh" (tea leaves)
Boiling water.

DESCRIPTION

Tea is the national drink of China. It replaces water and other beverages. It is the drink of the coolie and the millionaire. The purpose it serves is the same, and the only difference lies in the quality of tea leaves which are employed. In China two main types of tea are produced—*hsiang p'ien* (香片) or "Fragrant Leaf" and *lung ching* (龍井) or "Dragon Well" from the famous tea growing district near Hangchow. There are many grades of each, and prices vary accordingly. The quality of tea depends to a great extent on the size of the leaves, the top, or smaller ones being far more aromatic than the lower, or larger ones. The coarse, lower leaves, and even the stalks and stems are pressed into huge "bricks" which are much favoured by the Mongolians and Tibetans.

Writers of "Chinese cook-books" have endeavoured to throw a mysterious veil around the making of Chinese tea. Such theatricals are totally foreign to China. To make excellent Chinese tea proceed as follows :

PREPARATION

Keep a tea pot for Chinese tea only. After use rinse it thoroughly, but do not scour it. Tea is clean. Place a quantity of tea leaves in the pot, pour on fresh boiling water and allow it to set for five minutes. Do not add sugar, milk or cream, as the enjoyment of drinking Chinese tea depends entirely upon the aroma and not upon the stimulating qualities of tannic acid.

More boiling water may be added when the contents of the pot become reduced but it should be understood that the flavour and aroma will not be the same as the initial brew.

茶 鶏 蛋
10. CH'A CHI TAN
(Pronounced : chah jee dahn)
(TEA EGGS)

INGREDIENTS

　10 eggs
　4 oz. soya sauce
　3 oz. red tea (leaves)

DESCRIPTION

As a welcome and worthy change from hard boiled eggs, whether destined for the picnic, a salad, or hors d'œuvres "Ch'a Chi Tan" stands unrivalled.

PREPARATION

Fill a kettle with cold water to which has been added the tea leaves and soya sauce. Carefully place the eggs (after they have been thoroughly washed in cold water), in this mixture and place the kettle on the fire. When the water boils remove the eggs and put them in a pan of cold water. As soon as possible crack the entire shell of each egg—without removing any portion of it—replace in the tea mixture and again bring to a boil. When the eggs are a golden brown they should be removed and allowed to cool. The shells may then be removed, when they are ready to serve.

Approximate time of preparation: 15 min.
Enough for five people.

炒 鶏
11. CH'AO CHI
(Pronounced : chow jee)
(CHICKEN, SAUTED WITH CHESTNUTS)

INGREDIENTS

　1 small tender chicken
　½ lb. chestnuts (see note)
　½ cup soya sauce
　½ cup Chinese wine (黄酒)
　　(or sherry)
　2 tsp. lard

　½ tsp. ginger-root (薑)
　1 pinch salt
　1 tsp. sugar
　1 pinch aniseed
　1 pinch pepper

DESCRIPTION

Chicken prepared in this manner is welcome as a luncheon or dinner dish, or may be served with rice as part of a Chinese meal. The Chinese prefer to cut chicken in small pieces with a heavy, sharp cleaver (this does not fracture the bones), but the flesh may be removed from the bones if so desired and the chicken meat cut in pieces afterwards.

PREPARATION

Cut the chicken in small pieces, either with the bones or after the bones have been removed, wash thoroughly and dry between the folds of a clean cloth. Put the lard into a pan and when hot add the chicken and ginger-root finely minced. Stir constantly until the chicken has begun to brown, then add a pinch of aniseed. At this stage pour in the Chinese wine (or sherry), continue to stir for a few minutes, then add soya sauce, salt and sugar. Cover the pan with a tight lid and permit to simmer over a slow fire until the chicken is thoroughly done. Put in the chestnuts which have been parboiled, cook another five minutes. Place in a deep bowl for serving and sprinkle lightly with a small amount of black pepper.

NOTE : If chestnuts are not obtainable the heart of a cabbage, evenly diced makes an excellent substitute.

Approximate time of preparation : 45 min.
Enough for four people.

炒 韭 菜

12. CH'AO CHOU T'SAI

(*Pronounced : chow joe t'sy*)

(SAUTÉD YOUNG LEEKS)

INGREDIENTS

½ lb. pork, beef, or lamb   1 teaspoonful ginger-root (薑)
  (as desired)   3 tablespoonsful olive oil
1 lb. vegetable   4 tablespoonsful soya sauce
6 spring onions

DESCRIPTION

The word "ch'ao" (炒) in Chinese means either to sauté or to fry. "Chou t'sai" (韮菜) is the name of a vegetable, a member of the onion or leek family and is to be found in great abundance in the spring-time anywhere in China. Cabbage, spring onions, leeks, spinach, celery, string-beans, or almost any green vegetable desired can be substituted in following this recipe. The dish is usually served alone or with other similar dishes when rice forms the basis of the meal.

PREPARATION

The meat should first be diced quite fine, the vegetables and onions being chopped into thin strips not over 2 inches in length. Fry the diced meat, ginger (cut very fine), and chopped onions for about two minutes over a hot fire, using the olive oil for this purpose. Then add the vegetable and some water and cook with the utensil tightly covered. The time of cooking will depend upon what vegetable is used, though the average time to cook until done, would be between ten and fifteen minutes.

Approximate time of preparation: 25 min.
Enough for three people.

炒蝦仁竹笋

13. CH'AO HSIA JEN CHU SUN
(Pronounced : chow shah ren ju soon)
(SHRIMPS AND BAMBOO SHOOTS)

INGREDIENTS

1 lb. shrimps	2 tsp. lard
1 lb. bamboo shoots (竹笋)	1 onion (medium)
½ cup mushrooms	½ cup cooked peas
½ cup water-chestnuts (荸薺)	Salt and pepper

DESCRIPTION

This is a quick dish to put together and when served with rice makes an ideal luncheon.

PREPARATION

Boil and thinly slice the bamboo shoots. After draining well place the shrimps and the sliced bamboo shoots, minced onion, water-chestnuts (diced) and mushrooms in a pan in which the lard has been heated and fry for about five minutes, stirring constantly. Add enough salt and pepper to season and ½ cup boiling water. Cover and cook for a few minutes longer. Just before serving add the cooked peas.

Approximate time of preparation: ½ hr.
Enough for five people.

炒 肉 片

14. CH'AO JOU P'IEN

(*Pronounced : chow row pien*)

(PORK TENDERLOIN, FRIED)

INGREDIENTS

1 lb. pork tenderloin	1 tsp. olive oil
¾ cup Chinese wine (黃酒)	1 bud garlic
2 tsp. lard	1 tsp. rice flour
¼ cup soya sauce	¼ lb. ham
1 tsp. sugar	1 tsp. aniseed
2 cups soup stock	

DESCRIPTION

This is an ideal dish when served with rice—the two making a "complete meal." The ease with which it is made will also appeal to those who wish to prepare something quickly and make it at the same time very appetizing.

PREPARATION

Cut one lb. of fresh pork tenderloin into strips 1″ by 1″ by ¼″ in measurement. Place the meat in a deep bowl, pour over the wine and stir occasionally for altogether fifteen minutes. Wash in cold water and dry between the folds of a clean cloth.

Bring the lard to the boiling point in a pan and add the pork strips, stirring constantly with a pair of chopsticks. When turned a light brown add the soup stock, soya sauce and ham, aniseed and garlic. Do not cover the pan. When the liquid has been reduced ⅓ add sugar. Now put in the rice flour and when the mixture begins to thicken quickly add the small amount of olive oil. This recipe calls for a very quick fire, otherwise the meat is inclined to toughen.

When prepared by an expert Chinese chef it is most difficult to distinguish between pork and chicken.

Approximate time of preparation: ½ hr.

Enough for three people.

炒 麵

15. CH'AO MIEN

(Pronounced : chow mien)

NOODLES

IN EXPLANATION

For the benefit of the inexperienced it should be stated that "Ch'ao Mien" is a general term for all dishes in which fried noodles play the leading role. It would be quite sufficient merely to order "Ch'ao Mien" in any so-called Chinese restaurant abroad, and without a doubt some form of "Ch'ao Mien" would be prepared and served. Much would depend on the economic scale on which the restaurant was being operated, what foods were in season—and thus perhaps the cheapest—while the disposition of the cook and his love or dislike of industry would also figure as prime considerations.

In reality there are many different kinds of "Ch'ao Mien" and it may be of interest to list a few of the more important or popular varieties in both English and Chinese.

1.   **HUO T'UI CH'AO MIEN**
   (Pronounced : haw twae chow mien)
   大 腿 炒 麵

2.   **HSIA JEN CH'AO MIEN**
   (Pronounced : shah ren chow mien)
   蝦 仁 炒 麵

3.   **HSIA JEN CHI SSU CH'AO MIEN**
   (Pronounced : shah ren gee ss' chow mien)
   蝦 仁 鷄 絲 炒 麵

4.   **JOU SSU CH'AO MIEN**
   (Pronounced : row ss' chow mien)
   肉 絲 炒 麵

5.   **MO KO CH'AO MIEN**
   (Pronounced : maw gaw chow mien)
   蘑 菇 炒 麵

6.   **SAN HSIEN CH'AO MIEN**
   (Pronounced : sahn shien chow mien)
   三 鮮 炒 麵

7. SHAN SSU CH'AO MIEN

(Pronounced : shahn ss' chow mien)

蝦 絲 炒 麵

Thus, No. 1 is made with ham, No. 2 with small shrimps No. 3 with shrimp and chicken, No. 4 with sliced pork, No. 5 with mushrooms, No. 6 with ham, chicken, and sea slugs, and No. 7 with eels.

The preparation of any form of "Ch'ao Mien" demands two separate operations, i.e., the preparation of the "mien", or noodles, and the preparation of the ingredients selected to make any particular type of "Ch'ao Mien". One example is included in this volume, recipe number 27, under the heading HSIA JEN CH'AO MIEN (Shrimp) included in this volume.

A final item which might interest the reader concerns the use of "Chiang Yu" (醬油), or soya sauce as a condiment. In Chinese restaurants in foreign countries it is not unusual to witness diners saturating "Ch'ao Mien", and in fact all of their food with soya sauce. An extravagant use of soya sauce is considered by the Chinese an extremely unhealthy habit, as injurious as an over-indulgence in salt. It might be emphasised at this point that "Ch'ao Mien" cooked properly requires no further seasoning and additions of soya sauce can only tend to kill its flavor and render an otherwise crisp and appetizing dish a soggy mass.

炒 扁 豆

16. CH'AO PIEN TOU

(Pronounced : chow bien doe)

(STRING-BEANS AND PORK)

INGREDIENTS

1 lb. string-beans	1 tsp. minced onion
½ lb. fresh pork	½ cup soya sauce
1 tsp. lard	1 pinch salt
½ tsp. ginger-root, minced (薑)	

DESCRIPTION

When string-beans make their appearance in the spring-time in China it is rare that one will not find this dish on the tables of those Chinese who appreciate good things to eat.

PREPARATION

Remove the strings from the beans, wash carefully in cold water and break them in two. Bring the oil to the boiling point in a pan and fry the pork, which has been cut into ½ inch, cubes, until a light golden brown along with the small pieces of ginger-root. Then put in the soya sauce and 1 cup of boiling water. Add the beans, cover the utensil tightly and cook until the beans are well done. When almost finished add the pinch of salt, mix thoroughly and serve.

Approximate time of preparation: ¾ hr.
Enough for four people.

炒硫黃蛋

17. CH'AO SHU HUANG TAN

(Pronounced: chow shoo hwang dan)

(SCRAMBLED EGGS WITH SHRIMPS)

INGREDIENTS

6 eggs	2 tsp. lard
1 cup fresh shrimps	1 pinch salt
3 tsp. Chinese wine (黃酒) (or sherry)	1 pinch black pepper

DESCRIPTION

For a simple breakfast or supper dish, served either alone or on toast this is most appealing.

PREPARATION

With a pair of chopsticks or a mechanical whipper beat the eggs thoroughly. Add salt, pepper and wine, beat again and add the shrimps. Heat the lard in a frying pan and cook the mixture as one would scrambled eggs.

Approximate time of preparation: 10 min.
Enough for three people.

炒 五 香 肉
18. CH'AO WU HSIANG JOU
(Pronounced: chow woo sheang row)
("FIVE FLAVORED" BEEF)

INGREDIENTS

1 lb. lean beef	½ cup soya sauce
3 tsp. salt	1 tsp. sweet "chiang" (甜醬)
2 tsp. lard	(see page 55)
½ cup Chinese wine (黃酒)	1 pinch aniseed
(or sherry)	1 pinch black pepper

DESCRIPTION

Here is a dish which is most appetizing served either hot or cold. Once prepared and under proper conditions it may be kept for days. As a cold snack or a sandwich filling it is unusually good. Try it!

PREPARATION

Select a fine piece of lean beef and cut it into pieces about one inch square. Rub the salt in thoroughly. Heat the lard in a frying pan until piping hot, reduce the heat to medium, add beef and cook until slightly more than half done. Add the remaining ingredients and simmer until the beef is very tender. Remove, cool and place in a clean receptacle until wanted, or serve hot if so desired.

Approximate time of preparation: 1½ hrs.
Enough for three people.

炒 野 鴨
19. CH'AO YEH YA
(Pronounced: chow yeh ya)
(WILD DUCK)

INGREDIENTS

2 wild ducks	¾ cup soya sauce
1 cup bean curd	1 onion
¾ cup lard	1 tsp. "chiang" (醬)
½ cup Chinese wine (黃酒)	(see page 55)
(or sherry)	½ tsp. aniseed
1 tsp. salt	2 tsp. olive oil
2 tsp. sugar	2 cups stock, or water

DESCRIPTION

Wild game does not enter into the Chinese culinary art to any great extent, primarily because the flesh of wild animals and fowl is fibrous and therefore thought unpalatable. Wild duck is one of the exceptions to the rule however, and the following recipe insures a tender, savoury dish which is most appetizing.

PREPARATION

Place the lard in a deep pan and cook until piping hot, then add the duck which has previously been chopped with a sharp cleaver into one inch squares. (NOTE: It is essential that a *sharp* cleaver be used in order not to splinter the bones). Add the chopped onion, "chiang" (醬) and aniseed, and fry, stirring constantly over a slow fire for one half hour. Now add the wine and cover the pan tightly and simmer for another half hour. Put in stock (or water), soya sauce, bean-curd (diced), and salt, and bring to a boil. Just before removing from the fire add the sugar and olive oil and serve immediately.

Approximate time of preparation : 1½ hrs.
Enough for four people.

炒 油 蝦
20. CH'AO YU HSIA
(*Pronounced : chow yo shea*)
(SHRIMPS, COOKED IN OIL)

INGREDIENTS

1 lb. fresh shrimps	½ cup soya sauce
½ cup olive oil	1 tsp. sugar
¼ cup Chinese wine (黃酒)	salt to taste
(or sherry)	

DESCRIPTION

As a luncheon dish, to be eaten with rice, this is most appetizing. It may be quickly prepared. It is also recommended as a late supper dish when it may be served with thin toast.

PREPARATION

The shrimps should be carefully washed and cleaned, then dried between the folds of a clean cloth. Heat the olive oil to a boiling point in a frying pan, then add shrimps and the other ingredients in the order named. Cook until done and serve immediately.

Approximate time of preparation : 20 min.
Enough for four people.

鶏　絲　湯　麵

21. CHI SSU T'ANG MIEN

(*Pronounced : gee ss' tong mien*)
(NOODLES AND CHICKEN BROTH)

INGREDIENTS

½ lb. noodles
1 cup shredded chicken
3 oz. lard
¼ cup soya sauce
¼ cup Chinese wine (黃酒)
(or sherry)

onion, a little
ginger, minced, a pinch
salt, a pinch
1 cup water

DESCRIPTION

This is one of the simplest dishes to prepare and one which is as excellent as it is substantial. As a luncheon dish it can not be surpassed.

PREPARATION

Put the lard into a pan and heat it to the boiling point. Then add the minced chicken from which the skin has been removed. Cook a very short while and put in the soya sauce, minced onion and chopped ginger and Chinese wine (黃酒). Cook another two minutes and add 1 cup of boiling water, or enough water to thoroughly cover the *mien*, or noodles. When boiling hard, add the mien and cook until done. The noodles covered with the broth and chicken should be served while very hot.

Approximate time of preparation : 25 min.
Enough for four people.

餃 子

22. CHIAO TZU

(Pronounced : jow d'z)

(MEAT DUMPLINGS)

INGREDIENTS

1 lb. ground pork	1 ginger-root (薑)
6 spring onions	1 cupful soya sauce
2 tsp. olive oil	1 lb. cabbage
6 leeks	1 tsp. salt
1 cupful vinegar	2 cups flour
½ cup water	

DESCRIPTION

A "chiao tzu" (餃子) is really a form of meat dumpling—
a core of meat and vegetable surrounded by a light, thin
paste. They may be either boiled or steamed, and the
filling used can be varied according to taste. The above
ingredients are those commonly employed in Peking, where
"chiao tzu" are made best. Europeans and Americans
living in China consider that "chiao tzu" constitute a substantial meal in themselves, and it is rare indeed that other
dishes are served at the same time.

PREPARATION OF THE DOUGH

Place two cups of sifted flour into a bowl and add about
½ cupful of cold water. With a pair of chopsticks or spoon
mix the two thoroughly until they compose a very light
dough. Cover with a damp cloth and proceed with the com-
position of the filling mixture.

PREPARATION OF FILLING

Into one pound of pork meat chopped or ground very
fine mix six spring onions which have been chopped fine
(the green portion should be chopped as well as the white).
Chop a small piece of ginger-root very fine until the equivalent of ½ teaspoonful has been obtained and with one
tablespoonful of soya sauce add to the mixture. Then add
two tablespoonsful of olive oil and one pound of cabbage
which has been chopped very fine. The bleached portions

Making Chiao Tzu

of six leeks should then be chopped very fine and added to the mixture with one tablespoonful of salt. Mix all of the ingredients thoroughly.

DIRECTIONS FOR FILLING "CH'IAO TZU"

Flour a rolling pin and board as you would for biscuits. Now knead a small quantity of flour into the dough until it is quite dry but still plastic. Roll into a long thin string (about an inch in diameter). Pinch off uniformly small pieces about an inch long. Pat these once, but hard with the palm of the hand and you have a small flat cake. Roll each cake very thin with the rolling pin, trying the while to maintain a uniform circular shape. When finished each wafer should be about three inches in diameter. Place a heaping teaspoonful of the filling mixture on each cake, fold the wafer over once and press the edges together by pinching quickly with the forefinger and thumb.

DIRECTIONS FOR COOKING "CH'IAO TZU"

Bring a large pot of water to a boil. When boiling violently drop with care ten or fifteen "ch'iao tzu" into it and boil for eight minutes. With a perforated spoon or ladle remove the cooked "ch'iao tzu" from the water and serve immediately.

SERVICE

The table service for eating "ch'iao tzu" should include a bowl for each diner and both soya sauce and vinegar should be served. The two condiments may be partaken of separately or used together according to the individual taste. It is customary to immerse the "ch'iao tzu" into the liquid before eating. "Ch'iao tzu" are not good when cold and care should therefore be taken to maintain a supply of hot ones, removing those which have become cold and re-heating for a brief moment.

IN CASE OF LEFT-OVER "CH'IAO TZU"

Should there be left-over "ch'iao tzu" from the meal these may be kept, after cooking, until the following day. Then, fried to a golden brown, they make an excellent tiffin (luncheon) dish.

Approximate time of preparation : 1½ hrs.
Enough for six people.

煑 牛 肉
23. CHU NIU JOU
(Pronounced : ju new row)
(BOILED BEEF)

INGREDIENTS

2 lb. lean beef	1 small onion
1 turnip	1 tsp. sweet "chiang"(甜醬)
½ cup soya sauce	(see page 55)
1 tsp. sugar	1 pinch aniseed

DESCRIPTION

Particularly during warm weather this recipe for savoury boiled beef should have its followers. It is very simple to put together and makes a delightful dinner dish when served with individual portions of rice.

PREPARATION

Carefully wash and dry the cut of beef and place in a deep pan in which has been brought to boil sufficient cold water to cover the meat. Add the aniseed, sliced onion and sweet "chiang" (甜醬) and boil altogether for twenty minutes Remove the turnip from the pan, add the soya sauce and continue to boil for one hour longer.

Remove the boiled beef and place in a warming pan. Add the sugar to the broth and serve as a clear soup with the rice, or if preferred, chopped cabbage may be added, boiled until done, and served with the soup.

Approximate time of preparation : 2 hrs.
Enough for five people.

煑 神 仙 鴨
24. CHU SHEN HSIEN YA
(Pronounced : ju shun shien ya)
(BOILED DUCK)

INGREDIENTS

1 large, fat duck	1 onion
2 qts. Chinese wine (黃酒)	1 tsp. sweet "chiang" (甜醬)
2 tsp. salt	(see page 55)

DESCRIPTION

The name "Chu Shen Hsien Ya" means "boiled duck fit for the gods to eat." Whether or not the Chinese deities would really eat boiled duck is a controversial subject, but it is unquestionably true that duck prepared in this manner is most delightful and has the added attraction of being comparatively simple to prepare.

PREPARATION

Carefully prepare a good, fresh duck for cooking. Wash thoroughly, dry with a clean cloth. Place the minced onion and sweet "chiang" (甜醬) in the stomach of the duck. Bring the Chinese wine to a boil, add the salt and put in duck. Over a very slow fire boil the duck for six hours, tighly covered. Remove very carefully to a deep serving dish, pour over the broth and serve piping hot.

Approximate time of preparation : 6½ hrs.
Enough for four people.

煮 羊 肉
25. CHU YANG JOU
(Pronounced : ju yahng row)
(BOILED LAMB)

INGREDIENTS

3 lbs. lamb, or mutton
1 turnip
1 cup soya sauce
1 cup Chinese wine (黃酒)
(or sherry)

1 tsp. salt
½ cup sugar
2 stalks leek, or 8 spring
onions

DESCRIPTION

It must be remembered when reviewing a recipe such as this that the Chinese system of eating and arranging their menus provides always for some ample, wholesome dish which will prove "filling" as well as whet the appetite for more to come. Boiled food is usually considered commonplace abroad, and perhaps the reason lies in the fact that mere boiling with salt and pepper and a sliced vegetable or two marks the limit of the art. Served either as a course during a Chinese meal, or prepared as the mainstay of a foreign dinner "Chu Yang Jou" prepared in the following manner will be found more than acceptable.

PREPARATION

Select a fine piece of lamb, or mutton, cut into 1 inch cubes and wash carefully in WARM water. Put the meat into a kettle and pour over boiling water until the meat is half covered. Take a turnip, pierce it with a meat skewer and place it in the center of the meat cubes. Bring this to a boil, skim when necessary. Then remove the entire turnip. Add the Chinese wine and again bring to a boil. Then add the soya sauce and salt. Put the kettle over a slow fire and when the meat is done add the sugar. Five minutes before serving add the leeks or onions—not before. Serve piping hot in a large bowl, pouring over the sauce or broth just before serving.

Approximate time of preparation : 2 brs.
Enough for six people.

核 桃 鶏
26. HO T'AO CHI
(Pronounced : haw tow gee)
(CHICKEN WITH WALNUTS)

INGREDIENTS

1 cup shelled walnuts	2 tsp. flour
6 mushrooms	3 tsp. lard
1 cup chicken (diced)	1 tsp. salt
3 tsp. soya sauce	1 tsp. sugar

DESCRIPTION

"Ho t'ao chi", or chicken prepared with walnuts makes an excellent luncheon dish. It is also worthy of mention that walnuts prepared in the same manner that this recipe calls for, i.e., fried in deep fat and lightly sugared with confectioners' sugar, make a delightful change from salted almonds or peanuts.

PREPARATION

Fry the walnuts, which have been previously shelled and cleaned, in deep fat until they turn a golden brown. Quickly remove from the pan and blot on heavy manila paper.

Place the lard in a frying pan and when it gets good and hot pour in the diced chicken and fry for one minute. Have the flour, sugar, salt and soya sauce thoroughly mixed together, and pour this mixture on top of the frying chicken. Stir in the mushrooms (halved or quartered) and cook for about five minutes. Cover the pan, remove to the back of the stove, or to slow flame, and allow to simmer for a little while longer, or until the mushrooms are good and tender.

If desired, bamboo shoots, or a bit of chopped celery may be added. This is a matter of individual taste.

Approximate time of preparation : 40 min.
Enough for two people.

蝦 仁 炒 麵
27. HSIA JEN CH'AO MIEN
(*Pronounced : shah ren chow mien*)
(SHRIMP CHOW MIEN)

INGREDIENTS

½ lb. fine noodles
1½ cups small shrimps
6 oz. lard
1 tsp. salt
2 tsp. sugar

½ oz. olive oil
½ tsp. minced ginger-root (薑)
¼ cup vinegar
¼ cup soya sauce
½ cup Chinese wine (黃酒)
(or sherry)

DESCRIPTION

See CH'AO MIEN No. 15

PREPARATION

FIRST

Bring a large kettle of water to a boil and place the Chinese noodles, "Kua Mien" (掛麵), or foreign noodles in the boiling water, taking care not to add them so rapidly as to greatly reduce the temperature of the water. With a pair of chopsticks or a long fork move them about occasionally to prevent them from adhering to each other. When done remove them quickly from the water, place in a strainer or colander and pour over them immediately a kettle of cold water. Distribute them as thinly as possible on a damp (not wet) cloth and place them in a cool, airy place.

Place one-third of the lard in a pan and make piping hot. Add the shrimps which have been carefully shelled and cleaned and fry until a little over half done (about four minutes). Then add ¼ cup soya sauce, ¼ cup Chinese wine, or sherry, and 1 tsp. sugar. Cook another 3 minutes and remove from the pan and place in a warm place.

SECOND

Put the balance of the lard into the pan and make piping hot. Add the "Mien", or noodles, turn from time to time with a fork or chopsticks and fry until a golden brown. Now add the remaining soya sauce and wine, and salt, sugar, and minced ginger-root. Cook over a fast fire another two minutes, add the shrimps, cook another two minutes, and serve immediately.

Some people prefer a dash of vinegar on "Ch'ao Mien" and this should be provided at the table as its use is a matter of individual taste.

Approximate time of preparation : 1 hr.
Enough for four people.

黄 燜 鷄

28. HUANG MEN CHI

(Pronounced : hwang mun jee)

(SMOTHERED CHICKEN)

INGREDIENTS

1 fat chicken	4 oz. Chinese wine (黃酒)
4 oz. dried mushrooms	(or sherry)
(干蘑菇)	1 onion
2 oz. ham, minced	"Chiang" (醬), a little
4 oz. soya sauce	(see page 55)

DESCRIPTION

This is a recipe for smothered chicken à la chinoise. It is very simple to follow and the resultant dish will be found very superior to the ordinary "boiled chicken". It is excellent when served with either rice or *mien*.

PREPARATION

Take a fine fat chicken, clean and wash it thoroughly, and dry with a clean cloth or towel. Place the chicken, sliced onion, "chiang" (醬) and one cup of water in a kettle. Bring the water to a boil. Add enough water to cover the chicken and cover the kettle tightly. When half done add the salt, minced ham and soya sauce and mushrooms (which have been carefully washed) and simmer until well done. The chicken should be served in a deep bowl with the broth it was cooked in.

Approximate time of preparation : 1¼ hrs.
Enough for four people.

紅 煮 肉
29. HUNG CHU JOU
(*Pronounced : hoong ju row*)
(BOILED RED PORK)

INGREDIENTS

1½ lbs. pork	1 pinch arrowroot
1 cup soya sauce	1 small onion
1 cup Chinese wine (黃酒)	1 tsp. sweet "t'ien chiang"
(or sherry)	(甜醬)–see page 55
½ cup sugar	1 tsp. salt

DESCRIPTION

This is a dish with boiled pork as its basis. Served with rice it makes a most substantial and appetizing dish.

PREPARATION

Select a pound and a half of the finest lean pork and cut into pieces about ¾ of an inch square. Wash and dry between the folds of a clean cloth.

Put the pork meat, minced onion, sweet "chiang", Chinese wine, and soya sauce into a deep pan and bring to a quick boil. Add one cup of boiling water and cover tightly. Allow to simmer for two hours. Then add the sugar and arrowroot.

Approximate time of preparation : 2½ hrs.
Enough for four people.

紅 燒 白 菜
30. HUNG HSIAO PAI T'SAI
(Pronounced : hoong show by t'sy)
(CABBAGE COOKED WITH SOYA SAUCE)

INGREDIENTS

1 head cabbage	¼ cup Chinese wine (黃酒)
½ lb. pork (in 1 inch cubes)	(or sherry)
2 oz. mushrooms (dried)	1 tsp. sugar
½ cup shrimps (dried)	1 tsp. olive oil
4 oz. soya sauce	½ cup lard
1 bowl mushroom water	
(see text)	

DESCRIPTION

This is an excellent though simple dish to prepare and is usually eaten with boiled or steamed rice. Both shrimps and mushrooms can be obtained from any Chinese provisioner in dried form and may be kept in stock indefinitely.

Cabbage prepared in this manner is delightful when served as a vegetable with foreign food.

PREPARATION

With a sharp knife cut the head of cabbage into inch squares, wash thoroughly in cold water and drain off all surplus moisture. The dried mushrooms and dried shrimps should have been previously soaked in cold water, the water in which the mushrooms have been soaked being retained for further use.

Place one half of the lard in a deep pan, cook until piping hot. Add pork and fry until a light golden brown. Then add the cabbage, soya sauce, and sugar, and cook until the cabbage turns a rich red color. Remove the contents of pan and place to one side. Add the balance of the lard to pan and heat to the smoking point. Quickly add the soaked mushrooms (cut in any manner preferred), the shrimps and wine (or sherry) and bring to a quick boil. Replace cabbage and pork, add olive oil, water from mushrooms, cover the pan tightly and slowly simmer until the cabbage is thoroughly done.

Approximate time of preparation : 1 hr.
Enough for six people.

紅 燒 肉

31. HUNG LU JOU

(Pronounced : hoong loo row)

POT ROAST OF PORK

INGREDIENTS

2 lbs. fresh pork
6 oz. soya sauce
½ tsp. salt
4 oz. Chinese wine (黃酒)
  (or sherry)

4 oz. sugar
½ onion.
½ tsp. chopped ginger-root
water

DESCRIPTION

Instead of the conventional roast pork the following dish either with Chinese food or as the mainstay of a foreign meal will be found very appetizing.

PREPARATION

Select an excellent piece of tenderloin or another cut— not too fat—carefully wash and dry it and place it with all of the above ingredients (except the salt and sugar) in a kettle with a small quantity of boiling water. Simmer slowly for about 4 hours. Then add the salt and sugar, bring the liquid to a boil, skim carefully and serve.

Approximate time of preparation : 4½ hrs.
Enough for six people.

高 麗 蝦 仁

32. KAO LI HSIA JEN

(Pronounced : gow lee shah ren)

(SHRIMPS IN BATTER)

INGREDIENTS

1½ lbs. shrimps
¾ cup Chinese wine (黃酒)
  (or sherry)
¾ cup rice flour
½ cup soya sauce

4 eggs
1 tsp. pepper
1 tsp. salt
2 lbs. lard

DESCRIPTION

Shrimps or prawns prepared in the following manner never fail to tempt the most jaded appetite. The secret of their goodness however lies in their being served piping hot. Then they are lusciously crisp and full of flavor.

PREPARATION

Shell, clean and carefully wash the shrimps, being careful in the shelling to retain the tails. Dry between the folds of a clean, damp towel. Then place the shrimps in a bowl and pour over them ¾ cup of Chinese wine (黃酒), and allow them to remain in this for at least an hour. Add the salt to the wine after the shrimps have been placed in it.

When ready make a batter with the rice flour and the four eggs which have been briskly beaten. Add a little water if the batter is too stiff. Bring the lard to the boiling point and with a pair of chopsticks or kitchen pincers dip each shrimp quickly into the batter and drop in the hot grease. When a golden brown quickly remove. Place the shrimps on a warm platter (not in a bowl), sprinkle generously with BLACK pepper and serve instantly.

The soya sauce should be placed on the dining table, each diner serving himself according to his own fancy.

Approximate time of preparation : 1½ hrs.
Enough for four people.

烤蝦米麵包

33. K'AO HSIA MI MIEN PAO

(Pronounced : cow shea me mien bow)

(SHRIMPS ON TOAST)

INGREDIENTS

1 lb. shrimps	1 white of egg
1 onion, medium size	salt and pepper to taste
1 tsp. cornstarch	paprika

DESCRIPTION

Whether it be for the fish course of the formal luncheon or whether as the basis for that cozy little after-theatre party at home, this dish is supreme.

PREPARATION

Having washed the shrimps thoroughly the shells should be carefully removed and the whole meats then rewashed. Chop the meat very fine together with the onion, then add the cornstarch and the white of egg.

The bread should be carefully trimmed after being cut thin. Put a small quantity of the shrimp paste on each slice of bread, and fry them in a clear, deep fat until a golden brown. Drain thoroughly, garnish with a bit of parsley and serve piping hot.

Approximate time of preparation : 30 min.
Enough for four people.

烤 荸 薺

34. K'AO PI CH'I
(Pronounced : cow bee chee)
(BAKED WATER-CHESTNUTS)

INGREDIENTS

6 eggs	2 tsp. olive oil
1 lb. water-chestnuts (荸薺)	salt
1 cup milk	pepper

DESCRIPTION

The Chinese water-chestnut is a very appetizing vegetable and greatly favored by foreign residents in China. There are a number of ways of preparing them, or they may be eaten raw. The following method however is perhaps the most delicious of all.

PREPARATION

With a sharp knife remove the outer skin from the water-chestnuts and wash thoroughly. Cut in $\frac{1}{4}$ inch cubes. Mix the yolks of six eggs, milk, and olive oil and season with salt and pepper. Add the diced water-chestnuts and the whites of eggs well beaten and bake for about $\frac{1}{2}$ hr.

Approximate time of preparation : $\frac{1}{2}$ hr.
Enough for six people.

焗　子

35. KE TZU

(*Pronounced : gaw d'z*)

(THE CHINESE CHAFING DISH)

INGREDIENTS

1 small roast chicken	1 lb. ground pork, or
¼ lb. spaghetti	sausage meat
30 spring onions	1 ginger-root (薑)
4 tsp. cornstarch	1 cup soya sauce
6 garlic buds	1 pickled garlic bud (Note)
1 lb. rice	4 tsp. lard
1 lb. thinly sliced mutton	
or lamb	

DESCRIPTION

The term *kê tzu* in Chinese means chafing dish. This Chinese utensil is not dissimilar in construction to those used in foreign countries, with the exception of the heating unit. A flue, or chimney, penetrates the center of the native chafing dish and charcoal burned at the base supplies the necessary heat.

In this instance however, the word *kê tzu* denotes a food prepared in a chafing dish. The dish is particularly attractive and unique due to the fact that the diners prepare their own food, selecting from the variety of ingredients which surround the chafing dish. Individual bowls of rice are served the moment the food is cooked and serve as the basis of the meal.

Assuming that the meat balls, sliced chicken, onions, spaghetti, sliced lamb and soya sauce have been previously prepared and made ready, these dishes are placed around the chafing dish which occupies the center of the table. Chicken broth (this can be made from the chicken carcass after the meat has been carved away), or soup stock, is brought to a boil in the chafing dish. The spaghetti is then added. When the liquid again boils each diner selects portions of chicken, lamb, meat balls, onions, etc., and adds them to that portion of the chafing dish directly opposite to him. The length of time required to cook each item is very short and as the food is consumed, more is gradually added, thus maintaining a constant supply. More broth or stock can also be added, but care should be taken not to add too much toward the end of the meal as the concentrated soup which remains is very delicious when used to moisten the rice in one's bowl.

Although the above ingredients are those used by the Chinese there are undoubtedly other small vegetables which could be similarly employed, but this is a matter of individual fancy.

Attractive garnishing of the raw ingredients greatly adds to the appearance of the *kê tzu*, and the use of a modern chafing dish would overcome the inconveniences of the Chinese article.

NOTE

By "pickled garlic" is meant one which has been allowed to stand for some days in strong vinegar.

PREPARATION

To prepare meat balls for *kê tzu* proceed as follows :

Into one pound of ground pork or sausage meat mix thoroughly six spring onions which have been chopped fine (the tops of the onions should be used as well as the white portions). Add one quarter teaspoonful of ginger-root chopped very fine, four tablespoonsfuls of corn starch and one tablespoonful of soya sauce. Mix thoroughly and roll into little balls an inch thick. Fry to a golden brown in the four tablespoonsful of lard, piping hot. Arrange on a platter and garnish before placing around the chafing dish.

Approximate time of preparation : 2 hrs.
Enough for eight people.

辣 子 鷄

36. LA TZU CHI

(Pronounced : lah t'z jee)

(CHICKEN AND PEPPERS)

INGREDIENTS

1 frying chicken	1 tsp. salt
2 large green peppers	1 small onion
2 tsp. lard	1 tsp. sweet "chiang"
½ cup soya sauce	(甜醬)–see page 55
2 cups Chinese wine (黄酒)	1 tsp. vinegar
(or sherry)	1 cup water
2 tsp. bean flour	1 tsp. olive oil

DESCRIPTION

This dish represents the Chinese version of Chicken *à la King*, but instead of having a cream sauce it is made with a highly poignant sauce which is as unusual as it is appetising.

PREPARATION

Prepare the chicken for cooking by first washing thoroughly, drying between the folds of a clean cloth and dissecting as for fried chicken. With a sharp cleaver cut into pieces about 1 inch square, then with a sharp knife remove all bones.

Mix the bean flour with sufficient water to make a thick paste and dip the small pieces of chicken into this until well coated.

Have the lard at the boiling point in the pan, then put the pieces of chicken in and fry until a light brown. Then remove from the pan.

The peppers, from which all seeds have been removed and which have been carefully diced, should then be placed in the pan and cooked in the same fat until wilted. Replace the chicken, add the onion (minced) and sweet "chiang" (甜醬), soya sauce and Chinese wine (or sherry), sugar and salt. If necessary a little water may be added to keep the mixture from sticking. When the chicken is thoroughly done add just sufficient bean flour to thicken a little.

Approximate time of preparation : 1 hr.
Enough for four people.

栗 子 鴨 子

37. LI TZU YA TZU

(Pronounced : lee d'z yah d'z)

(DUCK WITH CHESTNUTS)

INGREDIENTS

1 large duck	1 cup soya sauce (醬油)
1 lb. pork, cut into	1 medium size onion
1 inch cubes	½ lb. chestnuts (small, whole)
½ lb. mushrooms	2 small pieces ginger-root

DESCRIPTION

In the art of preparing duck in many forms the Chinese are past masters. The dish described here is very simple to prepare and exceedingly delicious to eat.

PREPARATION

The duck should first be jointed and the pieces carefully washed and dried with a damp cloth. Place the pieces of duck in a large covered saucepan with the pork cubes, mushrooms, quartered onion, ginger-root and chestnuts. Add the cupful of soya sauce (醬油), and enough water to cover all. Let simmer over a slow fire until the duck meat begins to separate from the bones. Drain off the broth and save it for future use. Arrange the pieces of duck with the pork cubes, mushrooms and chestnuts, etc., on a platter and serve piping hot.

SUGGESTIONS

Either rice or noodles are excellent when served with the above duck dish. The broth makes an excellent soup or sauce and can be served with either one. Cold duck will be found to make a very delicious sandwich.

Approximate time of preparation : 3 hrs.
Enough for four people.

路 菜

38. LU T'SAI

(Pronounced : loo t'sy)

(DEVILED MEAT)

INGREDIENTS

1 lb. beef	½ lb. onions
½ lb. pork	1 tsp. "chiang" (醬)—see page 55
½ lb. sauerkraut	1 tsp. ground red pepper
1 tsp. soya sauce	1 tsp. lard

DESCRIPTION

This recipe hails from the city of Liangchou in the distant Province of Kansu. It is fundamentally a "travel ration", being prepared before the start of a journey and possessing qualities which permit of its being safely carried for weeks at a time. "Lu T'sai" may be used to embellish plain boiled "mien" or noodles, rice, or other cereals, and it is also excellent as a sandwich spread, or to form the basis of a rich, nourishing soup. For the camper, hunter or tourist there is no other prepared food which lends itself to so many different uses as Chinese "lu t'sai".

PREPARATION

With a meat grinder grind the onions, beef and pork separately. Put the lard in a frying pan and when hot add the onions and cook to a golden brown. Now add the beef and pork and cook thoroughly. When done add the remaining ingredients and cook altogether for a few minutes. Remove from the fire, and add ground red pepper and salt to taste. Pack in glass or porcelain bowls or jars, cover tightly and the "lu t'sai" is ready for use.

NOTE

Be generous in adding salt as this adds to the keeping qualities of "lu t'sai".

Approximate time of preparation : 1 hr.

木 須 飯

39. MU HSU FAN

(Pronounced : moo sh' fan)

(EGGS AND RICE)

INGREDIENTS (for one large bowl)

3 eggs	1 bowl chicken soup
$\frac{1}{4}$ cup Chinese wine (黃酒)	2 slices bamboo shoots
(or sherry)	2 small slices ham
3 tsp. lard	$\frac{1}{2}$ tsp. salt

DESCRIPTION

This is one of the most convenient and one of the quickest of all Chinese dishes to prepare. It may be ordered at practically any Chinese restaurant, on any steamship, railroad train or small foodshop with the assurance that within five minutes it will be served. Despite the rapidity of its preparation it is a most palatable and substantial dish.

PREPARATION

Put the lard in a pan and bring it to the hot point. Add the eggs which have been well beaten with wine and salt, and with a pair of chopsticks or a fork stir very rapidly for a moment until they begin to thicken slightly. Then quickly add the rice (which has been previously boiled and is thoroughly dry) and keep stirring. Put in one slice of ham (minced) add the chicken soup, and stir again until the dish is very hot. Remove from fire, place in a bowl, garnish on top with the remaining slice of ham and bamboo shoots, and serve.

Approximate time of preparation : 10 min.
Enough for two people.

釀 鷄 蛋 餃

40. NIANG CHI TAN CHIAO

(Pronounced : neong jee dan jow)

(EGG DUMPLINGS)

INGREDIENTS

5 eggs	3 tsp. soya sauce
$\frac{3}{4}$ lb. pork	1 tsp. salt
1 onion	1 tsp. sugar

DESCRIPTION

This is a very delicate dish which resembles the famous dish kown as "Chiao Tzu", only instead of the flour pastry of "chiao tzu" (餃子) a fine textured egg blanket is used instead. Care should be exercised in the cooking of this dish that the egg "rolls" are kept intact, as this adds greatly to their appearance when serving.

PREPARATION

The fresh pork meat and onion should be put through a meat grinder and to the mixture should then be added one tablespoonful of soya sauce and the salt. The eggs should then be beaten. One tsp. lard should then be dropped into a frying pan and when hot a large tsp. of the beaten egg is poured into the center of the pan much in the same manner as frying griddle cakes. Immediately place one tsp. of the meat mixture in the center of the egg, fold over, press down edges, and remove from pan.

When all have been cooked replace in pan, add ½ cup of water and the remaining 2 tsp. soya sauce and sugar. Cover tightly and cook slowly for ten minutes. If there is a tendency for the egg rolls to stick to the pan a slight amount of lard may be added at the time they are replaced in the pan.

Approximate time of preparation : 40 min.

Enough for three people.

牛 肉 青 菜

41. NIU JOU CH'ING T'SAI

(*Pronounced : new row ching t'sy*)

(CHINESE BEEF STEW)

INGREDIENTS

2 lbs. stewing beef	1 onion (quartered)
8 carrots	1½ cups soya sauce
4 potatoes	1 ginger-root (sliced) (薑)
1 bunch celery	8 spring onions (cut in 4 pieces)

DESCRIPTION

The possibilities of delicious beef stew did not escape the attention of the Chinese chef, and the following recipe elevates beef stew to an aristocratic status. It may be served with either rice, noodles, or pastry and will completely change your ideas regarding beef stew.

PREPARATION

Cut the beef into one inch cubes or squares and place them in a bowl or basin, covering them with cold water twice the depth of the beef. Soak for one hour or more. Drain the meat and place it in a saucepan with double the amount of water which should be boiling. Add 1¼ cup of soya sauce, the quartered spring onions, sliced ginger-root, and simmer over a slow fire (about 1½ to 3 hrs.) until the meat is thoroughly done. Remove the beef from saucepan, cover with enough of the liquid to keep moist, and place in a warming oven.

Place the quartered carrots, onion, potatoes and celery in the remaining liquid with the remaining ¼ cupful soya sauce. Cover and cook for about fifteen minutes, or until vegetables are done. Place the vegetables around the cooked beef, add sufficient of the sauce, and serve.

Approximate time of preparation : 5 hrs.
Enough for six people.

牛 肉 鬆
42. NIU JOU SUNG
(*Pronounced : new row soong*)
(SHREDDED BEEF, SPICED)

INGREDIENTS

2 lbs. lean beef
2 cups bouillon or
   chicken broth
3 oz. soya sauce

3 oz. Chinese wine (黃酒)
   (or sherry)
½ cup salt "chiang" (鹹醬)
   (see page 55)
2 oz. lard

DESCRIPTION

This extraordinary dish is sometimes served as an hors d'œuvre at a Chinese meal. It is also used to sprinkle on top of plain boiled *mien* or is eaten with rice. It is not difficult to prepare and possesses the advantage of long keeping qualities.

PREPARATION

Put enough lard (about half) into a pan to keep the meat from sticking. After removing all fat and tendons from the beef place it in the pan. Then add the bouillon or chicken broth, the salt "chiang" (鹹醬), wine, and soya sauce and boil until the meat is tender and the liquid is gone.

When the meat cools put it through a grinder and grind until very fine. Place the ground meat back in the pan with the remaining lard and cook over a very slow fire until dry. If placed in a clean container it may be kept for many days.

Approximate time of preparation : 1½ hrs.
Enough for six people.

白 菜 丸 子

43. PAI T'SAI WAN TZU

(*Pronounced : by t'sy wan d'z*)

(PORK MEAT BALLS WITH CABBAGE)

INGREDIENTS

1 lb. cabbage	2 cups water
2 lbs. lean meat	4 spring onions
(pork, veal or beef)	1 large onion
1 teaspoonful ginger-root (薑)	1 tsp. cornstarch
½ cup soya sauce	2 tsp. olive oil

DESCRIPTION

Pai t'sai (白菜) is the Chinese word for cabbage. *Wan tzu* (丸子) is the term given to meat balls; thus the combination of the two words is literally interpreted as meat balls with cabbage.

PREPARATION

Assuming that it is pork which has been selected to make this dish, the meat should be chopped or ground very fine. The onions and ginger, both of which have been chopped very fine, should then be added to the mixture along with the cornstarch. After mixing thoroughly the meat paste should be made into small flat cakes about two inches in diameter. Fry these in the olive oil until a golden brown.

Now shred the cabbage and distribute in a saucepan. Place the fried meat cakes on top of the raw cabbage and add the soya sauce, quartered onion and two pieces of peeled ginger-root. Add the two cups of water and cook over a slow fire until the cabbage is done. Drain the cabbage and arrange on a platter. Place the meat cakes on top and add a little of the liquid in which it was cooked. Serve hot.

Other vegetables could be served with this dish if so desired.

Approximate time of preparation : 1½ hrs.
Enough for six people.

爆 羊 肉
44. PAO YANG JOU
(Pronounced : bow yahng row)
(SAUTÉD LAMB AND ONIONS)

INGREDIENTS

1 lb. lamb, or mutton	2 onions, medium size
2 tsp. olive oil	½ cup soya sauce
½ tsp. minced ginger-root (薑)	

DESCRIPTION

This is a very appetizing dish when eaten with rice and has the additional advantage of being very easy and quick to prepare.

PREPARATION

Slice the lamb or mutton into very thin slices. Bring the oil to a hot point in a frying pan and add the lamb and ginger. Cook until the meat is well seared. Add the sliced onions and soya sauce, bring the latter to a quick boil and serve while very hot.

Approximate time of preparation : 15 min.
Enough for four persons.

日 本 菜 鍋 炮
45. SUKIYAKI
(BEEF AND VEGETABLES)
'A la Japonaise'

INGREDIENTS

1½ lbs. beef tenderloin
½ cup suet, or lard
1 cup soya sauce (醬油)
4 tsp. sugar
1 cup mushrooms

6 spring onions
1 large onion
1½ lbs. cabbage
½ cup bamboo shoots (竹笋)
rice

DESCRIPTION

In response to numerous requests this recipe has been included in this little volume. The dish is Japanese and not Chinese. As it is known so widely in the Orient and enjoys such great popularity with those foreigners and Chinese who have eaten and enjoyed it, its omission from these pages seemed hardly possible.

In Japan the preparation and serving of SUKIYAKI is a fascinating spectacle. The diners are seated on the mat flooring in front of a very low, circular table in the center of which is placed the "hibachi" (charcoal stove) or gas burner. Invariably the food is cooked and served by women, and the grace and skill of their operations presents a picture never to be forgotten. One's appetite is greatly stimulated while watching the process, and the fact that the cooking continues throughout the entire meal assures the food being served piping hot at all times.

PREPARATION

All ingredients should be prepared with a view to their being displayed on the table where the cooking takes place, i.e., in the most attractive and appetizing manner. Thus, the beef tenderloin should be carefully sliced in very thin strips about an inch wide and two inches in length. These should then be arranged on a platter and garnished with the sliced onion and spring onions. The cabbage should be sliced as thin as possible and arranged on another platter. The bamboo shoots and mushrooms, after careful washing and slicing, can be arranged on a third platter or used as a border around the meat.

If a chafing dish is to be used for the cooking it should be sufficiently deep to accommodate the raw materials required, it being remembered that only part of the ingredients are to be cooked at one time. The heating unit employed must also be of sufficient capacity to assure rapid cooking. If the actual cooking of the food is to be done over a gas or electric fire the vessel selected should be deep enough to hold all of the ingredients as in this case the sukiyaki would be prepared in the kitchen and served at the table.

METHOD No. 1. CHAFING DISH

Into the heated pan place the suet or lard. When piping hot add about half of the sliced meat and half of the sliced onion and spring onions. With a pair of chopsticks stir until the meat is well seared. Now add half of the cabbage, mushrooms, and bamboo shoots. When the cabbage has begun to wilt put in half of the sugar and soya sauce. Mix thoroughly and cover tightly, stirring occasionally until the cabbage is tender. A small amount of hot water may be added if the mixture appears too dry.

A bowl of rice should be served each diner immediately before the SUKIYAKI is served. Serving is accomplished by placing the desired quantity on top of the rice. When this is effected more of the raw ingredients should be added to the cooked food, the pan again covered, and the cooking repeated as in the first instance.

With the Japanese it is customary to break a raw egg over the top of each bowl of SUKIYAKI. This however is a matter of individual taste and the diners should be permitted to suit their own fancy.

METHOD No. 2. TO PREPARE IN THE KITCHEN

This process is identical with the foregoing with the exception that all of the ingredients are cooked at one time, the heat then being reduced to a point only sufficient to keep the SUKIYAKI hot after the initial service.

Approximate time of preparation : 1¼ hrs.
Enough for six people.

松 子 猪 肉
46.   SUNG TZU CHU JOU
(Pronounced: soong d'z ju row)
(PORK WITH PINE-NUTS)

INGREDIENTS

1 lb. fresh pork	3 oz. pine-nuts (松子)
½ pt. soya sauce	1 tsp. sugar

DESCRIPTION.

In the cool weather this makes a most excellent dish to be eaten with rice and has the advantage of being appetizing when served either hot or cold.

PREPARATION

Select an evenly marbled piece of fresh pork and with a sharp knife cut it into cubes about one inch square. Over a hot fire fry the pieces of pork for about five minutes, turning frequently. Add one pint of BOILING WATER, the soya sauce, and pine-nuts. Simmer the whole slowly until the pork is tender.

NOTE

Cabbage which has been previously boiled and carefully drained and on which the liquid from the above dish has been poured while piping hot will be found to be a most delicious accompanying dish.

Approximate time of preparation: 1 hr.
Enough for four people.

大 米 飯
47.   TA MI FAN
(Pronounced: dah mee fahn)
(R I C E)

INGREDIENTS

1½ lbs. rice

DESCRIPTION

There are perhaps hundreds of recipes for the preparation of boiled rice. Although the various processes differ somewhat, nevertheless the ultimate aim—to produce rice which is thoroughly cooked, attractive in appearance, and having each grain separate—is the same.

Two things are most essential, regardless of what process is employed. First, the rice itself must be of a fine quality. The rice grown in Korea is considered the best that can be obtained. Second, the utensil employed for the cooking of rice is very important. One made of a combination of brass and copper is regarded by the Chinese as ideal for the purpose. After reviewing several different methods favored by the Chinese the following has been selected as most satisfactory.

PREPARATION

Place the rice in a vessel containing lukewarm water and allow it to soak for one hour or more. Bring the kettle, filled with a generous amount of water, to a boil. Remove the rice from the first container and put it in the boiling water and cook for between twelve and fifteen minutes. At the end of this time remove it from the boiling water and place it in the first vessel, which has been cleaned and dried. After cleaning and drying the KETTLE replace the rice in it, place the kettle on the back of the stove and the rice will then "dry out" and each kernel separate itself from the others.

Approximate time of preparation : 1½ *hrs.*
Enough for six people.

糖 醋 蘿 卜

48. T'ANG TS'U LO PO
(Pronounced : tong dzoo law baw)
(RADISH SALAD)

INGREDIENTS

1 doz. medium sized radishes   ½ tsp. soya sauce
½ tsp. vinegar   ½ tsp. olive oil
½ tsp. sugar

DESCRIPTION

Although the Chinese chefs have not invented a repertoire of salads anywhere near as formidable as their Western contemporaries, still they do realize the importance of certain raw foods. Radishes prepared as follows is one of their best efforts.

PREPARATION

Cut one dozen fresh radishes in half after carefully washing and trimming them. Do not peel. Lay them face downward on a table and slightly crush each half with the flat side of a knife or other heavy instrument. Make a sauce of the vinegar, sugar, soya sauce, and oil and place the halves face downward in it, allowing them to remain so for one quarter of an hour before serving.

Approximate time of preparation : 20 min.

Enough for two people.

糖 醋 排 骨
49. T'ANG TS'U P'AI KU
(Pronounced : tong tzoo pie goo)
(SWEET AND SOUR PORK RIBS)

INGREDIENTS

1 lb. pork spareribs	4 oz. sugar
1 lb. lard	1 oz. soya sauce
1 oz. Chinese wine (黃酒)	1 tsp. salt
(or sherry)	1 cup water
2 oz. bean flour, vinegar (a little)	½ tsp. minced ginger-root(薑)

DESCRIPTION

This is the recipe for "sweet and sour pork", a dish which is usually featured in every so-called Chinese restaurant abroad. It may be served either hot or cold, though the former would seem to have the greatest number of advocates.

PREPARATION

With a sharp, heavy cleaver cut the spare ribs into pieces approximately one inch long and as wide as the bone happens to be. Wash in cold water, dry with a clean cloth or towel and dip immediately into the bean flour. Fry in the lard until a golden brown and remove quickly. Drain the lard from the pan with the exception of two tablespoonsfuls, replace the spare ribs and add the vinegar, the minced ginger-root, sugar, salt, Chinese wine (黃酒), soya sauce and the balance of the bean flour. Cover with one cup of boiling water and cook with the pan uncovered until the mixture "candies", or shows signs of becoming dry.

Approximate time of preparation : ½ hr.

Enough for four people.

糖 醋 魚

50. T'ANG TS'U YÜ

(Pronounced : tong dzoo yü)

(SWEET AND SOUR FISH)

INGREDIENTS

1 fish (about 2 lbs.)	2 tsp. sugar
¾ cup vinegar	¼ cup Chinese wine (黃酒)
1 tsp. rice flour	¼ cup soya sauce
salt and pepper to season	¼ lb. lard

DESCRIPTION

The widely known "sweet and sour" dishes prepared by the Chinese are particularly favoured by foreigners resident in the country. Certain meats and vegetables are prepared in the same manner, but fish, when prepared with the so-called sweet and sour sauce is exceptionally enticing.

PREPARATION

Carefully clean and cut a fine fish, about two or three pound in weight, and with a sharp knife make several intersecting incisions on both sides about one quarter of an inch in depth. Season with salt, pepper and a little soya sauce. Fry in the lard until good and brown on both sides and then remove the fish to a warm platter while the following sauce is being prepared.

Into the pan in which the fish has been fried put the vinegar, wine, sugar, the balance of the soya sauce, rice flour, a pinch of salt, and a cup of water. As soon as the sauce shows signs of thickening, pour it over the fish, garnish, and serve immediately.

Approximate time of preparation : 20 min.

Enough for four people.

PROVERBS

An eating-house keeper doesn't care how big your appetite is.

開飯店的不怕你肚子大

Better be hungry and pure than well-filled and corrupt.

寧可清饑不可濁飽

The more you eat, the less flavour; the less you eat, the more flavour.

多吃少滋味少吃多滋味

Whatever will satisfy hunger is good food.

物可充腸皆美食

Better that a man should wait for his gruel than the gruel should wait for him.

寧人等粥勿粥等人

Though boiled too much the meat is still in the pan.

肉爛了在鍋裏

Ducks in the Larder

CHAPTER IX

Ordering a Chinese Meal

FOR the benefit of those foreigners who do not speak the Chinese language, and as an aid to those who do, the following Chinese bill of fare has been compiled. It is believed that the list is fairly representative because it comprises a careful selection from the offerings of fifteen high and medium class restaurants in Peiping.

An effort has been made to provide as wide a variety as possible and with this in view the menus have been obtained from Peking, Shansi, Shantung and Southern caterers, and the masterpieces of each school have gone into the following compilation. It should be understood that in some instances there are restaurants which specialize in certain types of food. Thus, the famous "Peking duck", or *Hsiao Fei Ya* (燒 肥 鴨) as it is known in Chinese, reaches the zenith of its glory when prepared by the *Ch'üan Chü Te*, an old established restaurant located outside the Ch'ien Mên in Peiping. Notwithstanding this fact, a patron of a good Chinese restaurant may rest reasonably assured that his wishes will be met and his orders executed by any good restaurant, provided the edibles are in season.

And now just a word about the arrangement of the menu. It will be noted that the various dishes have been grouped under their proper headings. Thus, there is a section for fish, a section for duck, a section for vegetables and so forth. An index to the different groups will be found immediately following this chapter.

The description of each dish may appear to the reader to be rather brief. If so, it may be explained that to go into great detail concerning the ingredients, and the method of cooking every item would have amounted to setting down a recipe. Again, each restaurant has its own preferred method of putting together a dish.

The prices given are average prices only. A fluctuation of prices is bound to occur according to the season. The popularity, location, and management of a restaurant will also be reflected in its prices. As a rough guide to what one should pay, or may expect to pay, the prices quoted will answer the purpose.

In regard to the methods of cooking which are described it should be observed that thereare no less than 120 different Chinese characters or words denoting cooking processes. Thus, *Hsiao* (燒), *Cha* (炸), *Ch'ao* (炒), *Chien* (煎), etc., can only be translated into English as meaning to fry. The shades of difference are so obscure that they baffle description, and an attempt to be too precise could only result in confusion.

There are many times when a foreigner dining at a Chinese restaurant particularly enjoys certain dishes but finds himself totally at a loss to identify them when he wishes to repeat the experience at a later date. Space has been allowed between the items on the menu, and it is suggested that these be used for memoranda.

One must not rely upon literal translations of names to give the clue to what a dish really is. For instance, *Fei Ts'ui Kêng*, (翡翠羹) may be translated "jade purée" or "jade stew." *Fei*

Ts'ui Kêng is really a purée made from the lowly bean, but owing to its brilliant green color it has been glorified with the name by which it is known and thus raised from its humble rank into a realm of aristocracy and opulence. Many of the names do give some clue to the ingredients used, but on the whole they should not be relied upon.

It will be noted that certain dishes have beside them a star*. The likes and dislikes of foreigners eating Chinese food have been observed for many years and these observations have formed a basis for indicating those dishes which always call for appreciation. This does not imply, however, that the remainder are not appetizing or palatable. There is no accounting for taste, and the reader should be his own judge.

In conclusion it may be helpful to state that it is customary to donate 10% of the amount of the bill as a gratuity to the waiters. It is also usual to instruct the restaurant management to give twenty cents to the puller of each private rickshaw or fifty cents to the chauffeur of the car in which the guests arrive. The charge varies from city to city and is also dependent on the class of restaurant. This sum will be included in the bill when it is presented.

PROVERBS

Diligence and economy secure plenty to eat and drink; whilst idleness and sloth bring hunger and starvation.

勤儉勤儉茶飯隨便
懶惰懶惰忍饑受餓

To one who is warm enough in cotton clothes, and who likes his own ordinary food, the Book of Odes and the Books of History are always full of flavor.

布衣暖菜根香詩書滋味長

Farmers naturally realize enjoyment.

田家自有樂

Over a bowl of congee or rice one should remember the trouble it has cost to produce it.

一粥一飯當思來處不易

Viands have various flavours; what pleases the palate is good.

物無定味適口者珍

When rice is not well cooked it is because the steam has been unequally distributed.

飯不熟氣不勻

CHAPTER X

Dishes on the Menu

In the following lists, a cross reference (e.g., under No. 24. *Ho T'ao Chi* "See R. 26") is provided for all dishes described in the previous chapter of Recipes.

General Arrangement of Dishes served in Chinese restaurants grouped under their proper headings.

Classification				Page
Bean curd	豆腐粉	類	*Tou Fu Fên Lei*	106
Bêche-de-mer	海 參	類	*Hai Shen Lei*	107
Chicken	鷄	類	*Chi Lei*	107
Crab	螃 蟹	類	*P'ang Hsieh Lei*	110
Duck	鴨	類	*Ya Lei*	110
Fish	魚	類	*Yü Lei*	112
Flour or rice	麵飯食	類	*Mien Fan Shih Lei*	116
Fruit	甜 菓	類	*T'ien Kuo Lei*	117
Hors d'œuvres	冷 葷	類	*Lêng Hun Lei*	118
Liver, kidneys, tripe, etc.	腰 肚	類	*Yao Tu Lei*	121
Marine products	海 菜	類	*Hai T'sai Lei*	122
Meat	肉	類	*Jou Lei*	123
Mien, spaghetti, etc.	麵 條	類	*Mien T'iao Lei*	126
Pigeon	鴿	類	*Kê Lei*	128
Sheep stomachs	羊 肚	類	*Yang Tu Lei*	129
Shrimps	蝦 米	類	*Hsia Mi Lei*	129
Steamed dishes	蒸 食	類	*Chêng Shih Lei*	130
Vegetables	菜 蔬	類	*T'sai Shu Lei*	131

DISHES MADE WITH BEAN CURD

豆 腐 粉 類 *Tou Fu Fên Lei*

1. **Chi Ssu Ch'ao Fên*
鷄絲炒粉
Shredded chicken prepared with bean curd. $0.20

2. *Fa Chih Tou Fu*
法製豆腐
Bean curd prepared in the same manner as cooked in France (without meat). .18

3. *Hui Ko Shu*
燴割素
Bean curd and the skin of bean curd stewed together. .20

4. **Jou Ssu Ch'ao Fên*
肉絲炒粉
Shredded meat prepared with bean curd. .18

5. *K'ou Mo P'a Tou Fu*
口蘑扒豆腐
Bean curd cooked with mushrooms and seasonings. .16

6. *San Hsien Ch'ao Fên*
三鮮炒粉
Bean curd fried with chicken, giblets, and beef or pork. .20

7. *Shu Pan Fên*
素拌粉
Bean curd prepared with cucumber, sesame, and soya sauce. .12

8. *T'sui T'iao Fên*
脆條粉
Bean curd with beans. .16

DISHES MADE WITH BÊCHE-DE-MER
海 參 類 *Hai Shen Lei*

9. *Ma Chiang Hai Shen*
蔴醬海參
Sea slugs
$0.40

10. **Hsia Tzu Hai Shen*
蝦子海參
Sea slugs prepared with shrimp eggs.
.40

11. **Hsiao Hai Shen T'i Chin*
燒海參蹄筋
Sea slugs prepared with the tendons of pork meat.
.40

12. *Hu T'ieh Hai Shen*
蝴蝶海參
"Butterfly" sea slugs. Sea slugs stewed with seasonings.
.40

13. *Hung Hsiao Hai Shen*
紅燒海參
Sautéd sea slugs.
.40

14. *T'sung Hsiao Hai Shen*
蔥燒海參
Sea slugs prepared with leeks.
40

DISHES MADE WITH CHICKEN
鷄 類 *Chi Lei*

15. **Ch'ing Chêng Chi*
清蒸鷄
Steamed chicken served with a clear chicken broth.
$1.20

16. *Cha Chên Ch'ü Li*
炸肫去里
Fried chicken gizzards.
.28

17. **Ch'ao Chi Li Tzu*
炒鷄栗子
Chicken sautéd with chestnuts. See R. 11.
.80

18. *Chi Ssu Hui
    Wan Tou*
    鷄絲燴莞豆
    Chicken stewed with $0.32
    green peas.

19. *Chiang Pao
    Chi Ting*
    醬爆鷄丁
    Chicken cut in small   .28
    cubes and fried in deep
    fat.

20. *Ch'ing Cha
    Chên Kan*
    清炸胗肝
    Fried chicken giblets.   .32

21. *Ch'üan T'sui
    Chi P'ien*
    川脆鷄片
    Chicken sliced and   .32
    cooked until JUST
    done in boiling broth.

22. **Fei T'sui Liu
    Huang T'sai*
    翡翠熘黃菜
    Eggs cooked in chick-   .28
    en broth to the con-
    sistency of a cream
    soup.

23. *Fu Jung Chi
    P'ien*
    芙蓉鷄片
    Chicken prepared with   .36
    an egg sauce (similar
    to No. 22, *Fei T'sui Liu
    Huang T'sai*).

24. *Ho T'ao Chi*
    核桃鷄
    A delicious dish of   .80
    chicken sautéd with
    walnuts. See Recipe 26.

25. *Ho Pao Yin Ssu*
    荷苞銀絲
    Shredded white meat   .36
    of chicken prepared
    with a thin broth.

26. *Huang Men
    Chi*
    黃燜鷄
    Smothered chicken.   .60
    See Recipe 28.

27.	*Hui Sheng Chi Sun Ssu* 燴生鷄笋絲	Stewed chicken with bamboo shoots. $0.36
28.	**Juan Cha Chi* 軟炸鷄	Fried chicken (very tender). .36
29.	*Ko T'a Chi Chi T'sai* 焗燜鷄積菜	Chicken prepared with preserved vegetables. .48
30.	**La Tzu Chi* 辣子鷄	Small pieces of chicken stewed with red and green peppers. See Recipe 36. .40
31.	*Pa Pao Liu Huang T'sai* 八寶熘黃菜	Eggs cooked in chicken broth to the consistency of a cream soup, to which are added minced ham, chicken, vegetables, etc. .28
32.	*Sheng Chi Ting Fu P'i* 生鷄丁腐皮	Chicken cut into cubes, sautéd with bean curd skin, etc. .28
33.	*T'an Huang T'sai* 攤黃菜	Small omelets. .18
34.	*Tsao Liu Fu Jung* 糟熘芙蓉	Similar to No. 31, *Liu Huang T'sai*. .28
35.	*Ch'ao Huang T'sai* 炒黃菜	Scrambled eggs. .18

DISHES MADE WITH CRAB

螃 蟹 類 *P'ang Hsieh Lei*

36. *Ch'ao Hsieh Huang*
炒蟹黃
The "yellow" of crab, sautéd.
$0.48

37. *Chêng Ch'üan Hsieh*
蒸全蟹
Steamed crabs.
.48

38. *Jang P'ang Hsieh*
釀螃蟹
Picked crab meat steamed with various seasonings.
.48

39. **Liu Hsieh Huang*
熘蟹黃
The "yellow" of crab stewed in broth.
.48

DISHES MADE WITH DUCK

鴨 類 *Ya Lei*

40. *Ch'ao Hsiao Ya Ssu Ch'ia T'sai*
炒燒鴨絲搯菜
Shredded duck prepared with bean sprouts.
.48

41. *Ch'ao T'sai Hua Ya P'ien*
炒菜花鴨片
Slices of duck sautéd with cauliflower.
.28

42. *Ch'ao Ya Kan P'ien Ch'üan Tung T'sai*
炒鴨肝片川東菜
Duck livers sliced and prepared with Szechwan cabbage.
.48

43. *Ch'ao Yeh Ya 炒野鴨	Sautéd wild duck. This dish is seldom obtainable, but very good. See Recipe 19.	$0.80
44. Ch'ing Chêng Ya 清蒸鴨	Boiled duck served in a clear broth. See R. 24.	3.00
45. Ch'üan Chu Sun Ya Shê 川竹笋鴨舌	Ducks' tongues prepared with bamboo shoots and served in a clear broth.	.48
46. *Ch'uan Ya P'ien 川鴨片	Sliced duck boiled down in a duck bouillon.	.64
47. *Hsiao Fei Ya 燒肥鴨	The famous Peking roast duck.	3.00
48. Huang Lan Ya Yao Kuan T'ing 黃爛鴨腰管廷	Duck giblets stewed in white "chiang yu" or soya sauce.	.48
49. Hui She Chang 燴舌掌	Ducks' tongues and feet, stewed.	.64
50. Hui Ya I 燴鴨胰	The duck fat or grease, cooked with broth and seasonings and eaten on rice.	.40
51. *Hui Ya T'iao 燴鴨條	Stewed shredded duck.	.60
52. Hui Ya Yao 燴鴨腰	Stewed ducks' gizzards.	.48

53. *Juan Cha Ya Kan 軟炸鴨肝	Fried ducks' livers (soft).	$0.48
54. *Li Tzu Ya Tzu 栗子鴨子	Duck sautéd with chestnuts. See R. 37	.90
55. *Mien Pao Ya Kan 麵包鴨肝	Ducks' livers, fried and served on toast.	.36
56. Tsai Chêng Ya Kan 菜蒸鴨肝	Steamed ducks' livers.	.48
57. Tsao Ya Shê Nan Tou Fu 糟鴨舌南豆腐	Pickled ducks' tongues served with sliced bean curd.	.48
58. Tsao Ya Tou Fu Keng 糟鴨豆腐羹	Duck stewed with bean curd and served with a thick sauce.	.48
59. *Ya Kan Ch'ao T'sai Hua 鴨肝炒菜花	Ducks' livers fried with cauliflower.	.36
60. Ya Ting Fu P'i 鴨丁腐皮	Small pieces of duck stewed with bean curd.	.32

DISHES MADE WITH FISH

魚　類 Yü Lei

61. *Ch'ao Pao Yü T'sai Hua 炒鮑魚菜花	Abalone sautéd with cauliflower.	.80

62. *Chao Shan Yü P'ien* — Fried eels (in slices). $0.48

炒鱔魚片

63. *C'hao Shan Yü Ssu* — Fried eels (in shreds). .48

炒鱔魚絲

64. *Ch'ao T'sai Hua Pao Yü* — Abalone fried with cauliflower. .80

炒菜花鮑魚

65. **Chiang Chih Wa K'uai* — Fish fillets fried and seasoned with soya, etc. .60

醬汁瓦塊

66. **Chü Hua Yü Ko* — Fish prepared with the blossoms of the chrysanthemum — usually served in a chafing dish. 1.60

菊花魚焗

67. *Ch'üan Pao Yü P'ien* — Sliced abalone prepared in a clear broth. 1.20

川鮑魚片

68. *Ch'üan Wa K'uai Yü Lo Po Ssu* — Fish fillets prepared in a broth, to which is added shredded turnip, the fish being cooked until it is curled. .48

川瓦塊魚蘿卜絲

69. *Ch'üan Wu Yü P'ien* — Hunanese fish in clear soup. .36

川吳魚片

70. **Ch'üan Yü Chuan* — Rolls of fish in soup. .32

川魚捲

71. *Fu Jung Yü P'ien*
芙蓉魚片
Slices of fish prepared with an egg sauce. $0.32

72. *Ho Pao Yü Ch'ih*
荷包魚翅
Sharks' fins served with shredded cabbage, bamboo shoots, etc.   5.00 to 8.00

73. *Hung Hsiao Ch'ih Chin*
紅燒翅筋
Sharks' fins sautéd in soya sauce, sugar, etc.   5.00 to 8.00

74. *Hung Hsiao Li Yü*
紅燒鯉魚
Fried carp in a sauce made of soya.   .48

75. *Hung Hsiao Shan Tuan*
紅燒鱔段
Similar to the above, but cut in pieces prior to cooking.   .48

76. *Hung Hsiao Yü Ch'un*
紅燒魚唇
Selected portions of fish heads; prepared with a soya sauce.   2.40

77. *Hung Hsiao Yü P'ien*
紅燒魚片
Fish fried with a soya sauce.   .48

78. *Kao Li Yin Yü*
高麗銀魚
Whitebait prepared in the Korean manner.   .36

79. *Ko T'a Kuei Yü*
焗焗桂魚
Mandarin fish.   .48

80. *Kuei Hua Yü Ch'ih*
桂花魚翅
Sharks' fins prepared with a sauce made from the flowers of the cassia-tree.   5.00 to 8.00

81. *Liu Yü P'ien
    熘魚片
    Sautéd slices of fish. $0.36

82. Lung Hsü
    Pao Yü
    龍鬚鮑魚
    Abalone prepared with asparagus.   1.60

83. *Nai T'ang Pao
    Yü T'sai Hua
    奶湯鮑魚菜
    花
    Abalone prepared with cauliflower and served with a cream sauce.   1.20

84. *P'a Lan Ch'ih
    K'uai
    扒爛翅塊
    The finest dish prepared with sharks' fins.   6.00
                                                   to
                                                   8.00

85. P'êng Pao Yü
    烹鮑魚
    Boiled abalone.   .48

86. Sung Tzu Yü
    松籽魚
    Fish prepared with pine-nuts.   .64

87. *T'ang Tsu Yü
    糖醋魚
    Sweet and sour fish. See Recipe 50.   .80

88. Tsao Liu Kuei
    Yü P'ien
    糟熘桂魚片
    Mandarin fish served with a very highly seasoned sauce.   .36

89. *T'sui P'i Wa
    K'uai Yü
    脆皮瓦塊魚
    Sections of fish fried until the skin becomes very brittle and crisp.   .70

90. Wu Yü Tan
    烏魚蛋
    Fish eggs (of Black Fish).   .36

DISHES MADE WITH FLOUR OR RICE
麵 飯 食 類 *Mien Fan Shih Lei*

91. **Cha Ch'un Chuan*
炸春捲 — Fried spring rolls. — $0.02 a piece

92. **Chu Shui Chiao I Ke*
煮水餃一烱 — Boiled "chiao tzu" (meat dumplings). See Recipe 22. — 1.20 a bowl

93. *Chu T'ang Yuan I Ke*
煮湯元一烱 — Sweet dumplings served either with or without soup. — 1.20 a bowl

94. **Hun T'un*
餛飩 — Similar to *chiao tzu*, but served with a clear soup, and much more tender and delicate. — .35 a bowl

95. *K'ou Mo Ke Pa*
口蘑烱巴 — Mushrooms prepared in a baked *mo-mo** — .32 a bowl

96. **Mu Hsü Fan*
木鬚飯 — Eggs lightly scrambled and served in a cooked rice with minced ham, bamboo shoots, and broth. — .15 a bowl

97. *Pa Pao Fan*
八寶飯 — A pudding made from sweetened rice and containing various fruits, etc. — .60

---

*A *mo-mo* is a flat, circular baked bread made from wheat flour.

DISHES MADE WITH FRUIT
甜 菓 類 *T'ien Kuo Lei*

98. *Ch'ên Tzu Kêng* 陳子羹	The juice of the Fukien orange, sweetened and served warm.	$0.48
99. *Kuei Hua Shan Yao Tuan* 桂花山藥段	Potatoes sliced and prepared with a sweet sauce which candies when it cools.	.48
100. *Nai Tzu Shan Yao* 奶子山藥	Potatoes prepared with milk.	.48
101. *Pa Ssu Lien Tzu* 拔絲蓮子	Lotus seeds prepared in a heavy, sweet sauce.	.64
102. *Pa Ssu Shan Yao* 拔絲山藥	Potatoes diced and served in a heavy, sweet sauce.	.40
103. *Ping T'ang Lien Tzu* 冰糖蓮子	Lotus seeds served in a thin, sweet soup.	1.20
104. *P'u T'ao Kêng* 葡萄羹	The juice of grapes sweetened and served warm.	.48
105. *Tsao Ni Shan Yao* 棗泥山藥	Potatoes served in a thick sauce made from the Chinese jujube.	.40

HORS D'OEUVRES

Leng Hun 冷葷 "Cold Varieties"

106. *Chêng Pai Yü*
蒸白魚   Small, smoked fish, $0.36 dry.

107. **Chi P'i Ch'in T'sai*
鷄皮芹菜   Outer slices of chicken with celery (served as a salad).   .16

108. *Chiang Chen Kan*
醬胗肝   Chickens' livers and gizzards, sliced.   .28

109. **Chiang Chi*
醬鷄   Sliced chicken with *chiang*   .36

110. *Chiang Tu*
醬肚   Pig stomach, sliced.   .28

111. *Chiang Ya Pang*
醬鴨膀   Ducks' wings.   .36

112. *Chiang Ch'ing Ko*
醬青蛤   Small clams.   .36

113. **Ch'iang Tung Sun*
熗冬笋   Bamboo shoots, sliced.   .32

114. **Chih Mo Tun*
芥末墩   Shredded cabbage served with a sauce (*chih mo chiang*).   .15

115. *Ch'ing Pan*
清拌   Pig stomach cut very fine and served with a slightly sour sauce.   .28

116.	*Hsia Tzu Tu Fu Chu* 蝦子渚腐竹	Shrimps, bean curd, etc. served with a slightly sour dressing.	$0.20
117.	*Hsia Tzu Yang Ch'in T'sai* 蝦子洋芹菜	Shrimps and celery.	.16
118.	*Hsün Chi Ssu Yang Fên* 燻鷄絲洋粉	Finely sliced smoked chicken.	.24
119.	*Hsün Chi Tzu* 燻鷄子	Smoked eggs (without shells).	.24
120.	*Hsün K'ou T'iao* 燻口條	Smoked pig tongue sliced very fine.	.28
121.	*Hsün Sun Chi* 燻笋鷄	Smoked chicken sliced very fine.	.32
122.	*Hsün Yao Hua* 燻腰花	Smoked pig kidney cut in the form of small flowers.	.28
123.	*Huo Jou P'ien* 火肉片	Sliced ham.	.28
124.	*Nan Hsiang Ch'ang* 南香腸	Sliced smoked sausage.	.24
125.	*Niu Jou Sung* 牛肉鬆	Spiced beef, shredded. See Recipe 42.	.40
125a.	*Pan Ya Chang* 拌鴨掌	Pickled ducks' feet.	.48

126. *Pan Ya Shê* Ducks' tongues, pick- $0.36
拌鴨舌 led.

127. *P'ien Lu Chi* Sliced chicken, highly .36
片滷鷄 seasoned.

128. *San Ssu Yang Fên* Chicken, ham, bamboo .24
三絲洋粉 shoots.

129. *Su Tsao Yü* Small fish in oil and .36
蘇造魚 soya (Southern dish).

130. *Tsao Ya P'ien* Duck, sliced. .48
糟鴨片

131. *T'ang Hsin Sung Hua* Ducks eggs cooked .28
糖心松花 with an outer coating of mud, lime, etc. See Page 28—"Ming Dynasty" eggs.

132. *T'ang T'su P'ai Ku* Spare ribs with sweet .24
糖醋排骨 and sour sauce. See Recipe 49.

133. *Wu Hsiang Chi Sung* "Five flavored" chicken. .32
五香鷄鬆

134. *Wu Hsiang Yao P'ien* "Five flavored" pig .32
五香腰片 kidney.

135. *Wu Hsiang Yü* "Five flavored" fish. .36
五香魚

DISHES MADE WITH LIVER, KIDNEYS, TRIPE, ETC.
腰 肚 類 *Yao Tu Lei*

136. *Ch'ao Tu Ssu*   Fried pig stomach. $0.24
     炒肚絲

137. **Ch'uan Chia Fu*   A sort of potpourri   .40
     全家福   which includes pig
                             stomach, ham, chicken,
                             chicken fillets, etc.

138. *Ch'uan Shuang*   A dish prepared with   .32
     T'sui   various intestines and
     川雙脆   served with a broth.

139. *Hui San Hsien*   A stew made from   .30
     燴三鮮   various intestines.

140. **Juan Chao Yao*   Pig kidneys sliced and   .30
     Hua   cut in the form of
     軟炸腰花   flowers and fried until
                             soft.

141. *Kan Pei Tu*   Pig stomach, cut into   .32
     K'uai   pieces and prepared
     干貝肚塊   with cockles.

142. *P'a Kuan T'ing*   Pig intestines prepar-   .32
     Fu Chu   ed with bean curd and
     扒管廷腐竹   bamboo shoots.

143. *T'ang Pao Tu*   Pig stomach in soup.   .32
     Jên
     湯爆肚仁

144. *Yao Ting Fu*   Pig kidney and bean   .28
     P'i   curd skin.
     腰丁腐皮

145. *Yen Pao Kuan T'ing*
鹽爆管廷
Intestines cooked in a salted broth.
$0.38

146. *Yen Pao Tu Jên*
鹽爆肚仁
Pig stomachs sliced and cooked in a salted broth.
.32

147. *Yu Pao Shuang T'sui*
油爆雙脆
Pig stomach and chicken gizzard.
.32

148. *Yu Pao Tu Jên*
油爆肚仁
Pig stomach sliced and cooked in oil.
.32

DISHES MADE WITH MARINE PRODUCTS
海 菜 類 *Hai T'sai Lei*

149. **Ch'ing T'ang Yen Wo*
清湯燕窩
Birds'-nest soup.
$3.00

150. *Ko Jên Tou Fu Kêng*
蛤仁豆腐羹
A thick stew made from small clams and bean curd.
.36

151. *Kuei Hua Kan Pei*
桂花干貝
Winkles.
.32

152. *Pai Mu Erh
白木耳
White fungi, stewed or sautéd.
1.00

153. *Pan Hai Chê*
拌海蜇
Ocean jelly-fish.
.30

DISHES MADE WITH MEAT

肉 類 *Jou Lei*

154. **Cha Fên Jou P'ien* 炸粉肉片 — Pork cutlets fried in batter. See Recipe 4. $0.45

155. **Cha Huo T'ui Yuan* 炸火腿圓 — Ham and eggs prepared in a highly appetizing manner. See R. 5. .30

156. *Cha T'sai Ch'ao Jou Ssu* 榨菜炒肉絲 — Vegetables fried with pork, specially prepared in Southern China. .28

157. **Cha Wan Tzu* 炸丸子 — Pork meat balls fried in deep fat. See R. 1. .20

158. *Chao Yen Chou Tzu* 椒鹽肘子 — Pork joints, steamed. .52

159. **Ch'ao Jou Ssu* 炒肉絲 — Fried slices of pork meat. See Recipe 14. .26

160. **Ch'ao Niu Jou P'ien* 炒牛肉片 — Fried small slices of beef. .28

161. **Ch'ao Niu Jou Ssu* 炒牛肉絲 — Fried slices of beef. .28

162. **Ch'ao Wu Hsiang Jou* 炒五香肉 — "Five flavoured" beef. A highly seasoned dish. See Recipe 18. .75

163. *Chiang Pao Li Chi Ting* 醬爆里几丁 — Pork tenderloin fried with soya sauce and other seasonings. .28

164.	*Chu Yang Jou 煨羊肉	Boiled mutton. See Recipe 25.	$0.50
165.	Ch'üan Wan Tzu 川丸子	Small pork balls served in soup.	.28
166.	Fo Shou Ch'ao Jou Ssu 佛手炒肉絲	Pork prepared with citrus fruits.	.28
167.	Ho Yeh Jou 荷葉肉	Pork meat seasoned and steamed beneath leaves of the lotus plant.	.35
168.	Hsia Tzu T'i Chin 蝦子蹄筋	Small slices of pork fried with shrimps.	.30
169.	Hung Hsiao T'i Chin 紅燒蹄筋	Small slices of pork fried and seasoned with soya sauce and other seasonings.	.30
170.	Hung Hsiao Chou Tzu 紅燒肘子	Joints of pork fried and seasoned with spices and soya sauce.	.52
171.	*Hung Hsiao Jou 紅燒肉	Selected bits of pork meat fried and season- ed with soya sauce, etc. See Recipe 29.	.35
172.	*Hung Hsiao Niu Jou 紅燒牛肉	Selected bits of beef fried and seasoned with soya sauce, etc.	.25
173.	*Hung Lu Jou 紅燜肉	A Chinese version of pot roast of pork. See Recipe 31.	.50

174. *I P'in Jou*
一品肉
A beef tenderloin whole or portion beef tenderloin fried with soya sauce, etc. served without being previously sliced.
$0.30

175. **Kê Tzu*
焗子
The famous mutton dish prepared at the table with a chafing dish. See Recipe 35.
2.00

176. *Kê T'a Jou*
焗爛肉
Pork or beef, smothered. See Recipe 41.
.28

177. **Liu Jou P'ien*
熘肉片
Sautéd pork.
.24

178. **La Tzu Jou Ting*
辣子肉丁
Sliced pork sautéd with green peppers.
.28

179. *Liu Wan Tzu*
熘丸子
Pork balls sautéd in a highly seasoned sauce.
.30

180. **Mi Fên Jou*
米粉肉
Pork sliced and smothered in a thick sauce thickened with rice flour.
.36

181. **Mu Hsü Jou*
木鬚肉
Lightly scrambled eggs to which have been added small bits of fried pork. See R. 39.
.28

182. *Nan K'ou Jou*
南扣肉
Small cubes of very fat pork, fried crisp on the outside and seasoned with pepper and soya sauce.
.30

183. *P'ao T'sai Ch'ao Jou Mo* 泡菜炒肉未   Pickled vegetables (usually from South China) prepared with fried pork. $0.22

184. *Shui Ching Chou Tzu* 水晶肘子   Pork joints, boiled with various seasonings. (Eaten cold).   .52

185. **Tung T'sai Ch'ao Jou Ssu* 冬菜炒肉絲   Pork sautéd with cabbage and other winter vegetables.   .28

186. **Tun Niu Jou* 燉牛肉   Beef simmered with various sauces and seasonings until very tender. See Recipe 23.   .28

187. *Yü Lan Ch'ao Jou Ssu* 玉蘭炒肉絲   Minced pork sautéd with the sliced shoots of the *yulan* or Magnolia.   .28

DISHES MADE WITH MIEN

麵 條 類 *Mien T'iao Lei*

188. *Cha Chiang Mien* 炸醬麵   *Mien* prepared with a thick, spicy sauce. See Recipe 3.   .60

189. **Chi Ssu T'ang Mien* 鷄絲湯麵   Thin noodles cooked in a clear broth and garnished with sliced chicken. See Recipe 21.   .10

190. *Ch'uan Lu Pan Mien* 全滷拌麵   Thin noodles cooked in a pork broth later thickened with beaten egg, to which is added mushrooms, minced chicken, bamboo shoots, etc.   .40

191. *Huo T'ui
    Ch'ao Mien
    火腿炒麵
Thin noodles fried with ham, soya sauce, mushrooms, etc. — $0.14

192. *Hsia Jên
    Ch'ao Mien
    蝦仁炒麵
Thin noodles fried with small shrimps. See Recipe 27. — .14

193. *Hsia Jên Chi
    Ssu Ch'ao
    Mien
    蝦仁鷄絲
    炒麵
Thin noodles fried with small shrimps and chicken. See R. 15. — .18

194. *Hsia Jen
    T'ang Mien
    蝦仁湯麵
Thin noodles cooked in a clear broth and with small shrimps. — .12

195. I Fu Mien
    伊府麵
Broad noodles prepared in a rich chicken broth, lightly seasoned, and enriched with the white meat of chicken, mushrooms, and shredded ham. — .20

196. *Jou Ssu Ch'ao
    Mien
    肉絲炒麵
Thin noodles fried with small slices of pork, soya sauce, etc. See Recipe 15. — .12

197. *Jou Ssu T'ang
    Mien
    肉絲湯麵
Thin noodles cooked in broth with small slices of pork meat. — .10

198. *Niu Jou T'ang
    Mien
    牛肉湯麵
Thin noodles cooked in broth with small slices of beef. — .12

199. *San Hsien Pan Mien* 三鮮拌麵 — Thin noodles cooked in broth and mixed with minced ham, chicken, etc., etc. $0.14

200. **San Hsien Ch'ao Mien* 三鮮炒麵 — Thin noodles fried and mixed with minced ham, chicken, bamboo shoots, etc. See R. 15. .14

201. **San Hsien T'ang Mien* 三鮮湯麵 — Thin noodles cooked in broth and served with the broth with which has been mixed minced ham, chicken, etc. .12

202. *Shan Ssu Ch'ao Mien* 鱔絲炒麵 — Fried noodles with small slices of fried eel. See Recipe 15. .16

203. *Shan Ssu T'ang Mien* 鱔絲湯麵 — Thin noodles cooked in broth with small slices of eel. .12

DISHES MADE WITH PIGEON

鴿 類 *Ke Lei*

204. *Fu Jung Ke Tan* 芙蓉鴿蛋 — Pigeon eggs cooked in broth and a small amount of beaten egg and seasoning, and served in a small quantity of the sauce. .48

205. **Hung Hsiao Kê Tan* 紅燒鴿蛋 — Pigeon eggs sautéd with soya sauce and seasonings. .48

DISHES MADE WITH SHEEPS' STOMACHS
羊 肚 類 *Yang Tu Lei*

206. *Ch'ao Kuan T'ing Yang Tu Hsin*
炒管廷羊肚菌
Fried sheep intestines and stomach. $0.32

207. *Ch'uan Ching Tsan Tan*
川淨散旦
Sheep tripe in broth.   .32

208. **Hung Hsiao Yang Tu Hsin*
紅燒羊肚菌
Sheep stomach sautéd with soya sauce and a cheap type of mushroom commonly eaten in China.   .28

209. *Shu Hsiao Yang Tu Mo*
素燒羊肚末
Sheep stomach prepared with mushrooms and a clear sauce.   .24

DISHES MADE WITH SHRIMPS
蝦 類   *Hsia Lei*

210. **Cha Hsia Ch'ien*
炸蝦肨
Fried shrimps (the large ones).   .32

211. **Cha Hsia Ch'iu Erh*
炸蝦球兒
Small shrimp balls fried in deep fat. See R. 6.   .40

212. *Chia Hsia T'o*
炸蝦坨
Fried shrimps (the small ones). See R. 20.   .36

213. **Ch'ao Hsia Jen Chu Sun*
炒蝦仁竹笋
Shrimps sautéd with bamboo shoots. See Recipe 13.   .30

214.	*Ch'ao Hsia P'ien* 炒蝦片	Fried prawns, in slices.	$0.36
215.	*Fu Jung Hsia P'ien* 芙蓉蝦片	Prawns stewed with an egg sauce.	.36
216.	*Hsia Tzu T'a Tou Fu* 蝦子燜豆腐	Prawn eggs prepared with bean curd.	.24
217.	*Hui Hsia Jên* 燴蝦仁	Small shrimps, stewed.	.48
218.	*Juan Cha Hsia Jên* 軟炸蝦仁	Small shrimps fried in an egg batter. See Recipe 32.	.36
219.	*Mien Pao Hsia Jên* 麵包蝦仁	Small shrimps fried, and served on toast. See Recipe 33.	.36
220.	*Nan Chien Hsiao Hsia Ping* 南煎小蝦餅	Small shrimps with pastry wafers.	.36
221.	*P'êng Tui Hsia* 烹對蝦	Prawns sautéd with a high seasoning.	.36

STEAMED DISHES

蒸 食 類 *Chêng Shih Lei*

222.	*Hsiao Mai* 燒賣	A steamed dumpling, crimped at the top.	.01 apiece
223.	*Jou Hsien Pao* 肉餡包	A type of dumpling stuffed with meat and/or vegetable and steamed until done.	.01 apiece

224. *Nai Yu San Hsien Chuan* 奶油三鮮捲   A pastry roll, stuffed usually with ham, chicken, etc., steamed until done, and sliced into portions. $0.32

225. *Shui Ching Pao* 水晶包   A type of dumpling stuffed with vegetables, seasoned with spices and oils, and steamed.   .01 apiece

226. *T'ang Mien Chiao* 湯麵餃   Steamed dumplings, very similar to No. 223, *Jou Hsien Pao*   .01 apiece

227. *Tsao Ni Fang P'u* 棗呢方圃   Steamed small rolls stuffed with a sweet paste made from Chinese jujubes.   .24

228. *T'suan Hsien Pao Tzu* 攢餡包子   Dumplings, stuffed with meat and vegetables, and steamed.   .02 apiece

DISHES MADE WITH VEGETABLES
菜 蔬 類 *T'sai Shu Lei*

229. *Ch'ao Chou T'sai* 炒韭菜   Young leeks sautéd with pork. See R. 12.   .30

230. *Ch'ao Hsiang Ku Sun P'ien* 炒香菇笋片   Bamboo shoots and two kinds of mushrooms, sautéd.   .32

231. *Ch'ao Pien Tou* 炒扁豆   Young string-beans sautéd with sliced pork, ginger, etc. See R. 16.   .30

232. *Ch'ao San Pai*   Mushrooms, water- $0.40
     炒三白   chestnuts, cabbage,
              bamboo shoots, or any
              WHITE vegetables,
              sautéd.

233. *Ch'ao Ssu*   A southern vegetable,   .28
     T'sai T'ai   resembling cabbage,
     炒紫菜台   purple in color, sautéd.

234. *Ch'uan Chen*   Small mushrooms cook-   .48
     Chu° Mo   ed and served in a
     川珍珠蘑   clear soup.

235. *Ch'ing La Chiao*   Green peppers and   .28
     Ch'ao Mao   small green beans saut-
     Tou   éd together.
     青辣椒炒
     毛豆

236. *Ch'üan Pai Chu*   Bamboo shoots pre-   .60
     Sun   pared and served in
     川白竹笋   a clear soup.

237. *Ch'uan Yang*   A clear asparagus soup.   .60
     Lung Hsü
     川洋龍鬚

238. *Fei T'sui Kêng*   A puree made from a   .36
     翡翠羹   type of large Lima bean.

239. *Huo T'ui Ch'ao*   Cauliflower sautéd with   .32
     T'sai Hua   ham.
     火腿炒菜花

240. *Hsia Mi Ch'ao*   Small shrimps sautéd   .20
     Yu T'sai   with rape.
     蝦米炒油菜

241. *Hsia Tzu Chiao Pai* — Watercress sautéd with shrimp eggs. — $0.28

蝦子茭白

242. *Hsia Tzu Ch'un Sun* — Southern bamboo shoots sautéd with shrimp eggs. — .32

蝦子春笋

243. *Hsia Tzu Yü Lan P'ien* — Bamboo shoots prepared with shrimp eggs (similar to No. 242, *Hsia Tzu Ch'un Sun*). — .32

蝦子玉蘭片

244. *Ch'ao Chiao Pai* — Watercress, sautéd. — .28

炒茭白

245. *Hsieh Huang Hsiao Pai T'sai* — Crab "yellow" sautéd with white cabbage. — .24

蟹黃燒白菜

246. *Hsieh Huang Tung Sun* — Bamboo shoots sautéd with crab "yellow." — .32

蟹黃冬笋

247. *Hui Hsien Mo* — Stewed fresh mushrooms. — .48

燴鮮蘑

248. *Hung Hsiao Hsien Mo* — Fresh mushrooms sautéd with soya sauce and other seasonings. — .48

紅燒鮮蘑

249. *Hung Hsiao Kan Pei Lo Po Ch'iu* — Winkles and turnip minced, made into small balls, then fried and simmered in a seasoned sauce. — .36

紅燒干貝羅卜球

250. *Hung Hsiao Pai T'sai* — Smothered cabbage. See Recipe 30. — .30

紅燒白菜

251. *Hung Hsiao
   Tung Sun*
   紅燒冬笋

   Bamboo shoots sautéd in soya sauce.

   $0.48

252. **K'ou Mo Hsiao
   Pai T'sai*
   口蘑燒白菜

   Cabbage sautéd with mushrooms.

   .24

253. *K'ou Mo Hsiao
   Ssu Kua*
   口蘑燒絲瓜

   "Ssu kua" (a vegetable resembling a large cucumber) sautéd with mushrooms.

   .20

254. **Li Tzu Hsiao
   Pai T'sai*
   栗子燒白菜

   Cabbage sautéd with chestnuts.

   .20

255. *Mao Tou Hsiao
   Ch'ieh Tzu*
   毛豆燒茄子

   Eggplant sautéd with green beans.

   .28

256. **Nai T'ang
   Lung Hsu
   T'sai Hua*
   奶湯龍鬚菜花

   Asparagus and cauliflower prepared with a milk sauce.

   .80

257. **Nai T'ang Pai
   T'sai*
   奶湯白菜

   Creamed cabbage.

   .28

258. **Nai T'ang
   T'sai Hua*
   奶湯菜花

   Creamed cauliflower.

   .32

259. **Nai T'ang
   Tung Sun*
   奶湯冬笋

   Creamed bamboo shoots.

   .48

260. **Pai T'sai
   Wan Tzu*
   白菜丸子

   Pork meat balls with cabbage. See R. 43.

   .60

PROVERBS

The house of a well-to-do man is indicated by the presence of the following,—fuel, rice, oil, salt, sauce, vinegar and tea.

柴米油鹽醬醋茶七字安排好人家

Anywhere in the world salt is good to eat; anywhere in the world money is good to use.

吃盡天下鹽好用盡天下錢好

Clothes and food are daily mercies.

衣飯逐日生

He who sows hemp will reap hemp, he who sows beans will reap beans.

種蔴得蔴種豆得豆

CHAPTER XI

English-Chinese Dictionary of Foodstuffs

IN compiling the following English-Chinese dictionary of foodstuffs an effort has been made to make the list as complete as possible; but certain limitations are recognized. There are many products and edibles unknown to the Chinese, such as currants, gooseberries and tapioca. True, foreigners have from time to time imported the plants or seeds of fruits, flowers, and vegetables unknown to China, and in these cases the Chinese to whose attention they have been drawn have improvised terms which have served to identify them. Such names as they have invented are certainly not universally known, and therefore their inclusion in a book such as this would only tend to confuse or mystify.

Certain foods enjoy two or more names, while others are known by different names in different localities. Perhaps the humble potato is known by more names than any other vegetable in China. *Shan yao* (山藥), *shan yao tou* (山藥豆), *t'u tou* (土豆), *ti tou* (地豆), *shan tou* (山豆), *ku tzu* (谷子) and *t'u erh* (土兒) all mean POTATO somewhere in this mighty land. An effort has therefore been made in each case to reduce all terms to their common denominator and thus avoid cluttering up the Chinese text with a number of uncertain words. A space has been provided in the index for the recording of local names, and through this medium it is hoped to provide a way out of a difficult problem.

The Romanization of all Chinese names follows the Wade system. No attempt has been made to employ an additional simplified spelling, because first, without a knowledge of tone values it is doubtful whether those unable to speak the Chinese language could make themsleves clear, and second, because the inclusion of the Chinese characters provides a simple means of communicating one's wishes.

Allspice	*ko hsiang liao*	各香料
Almond	*hsing jen*	杏仁
Aniseed	*hui hsiang*	茴香
Apple	*p'in kuo*	蘋菓
Apricot	*hsing erh*	杏兒
„ seeds	*hsing jen*	杏仁
Arrowroot	*ou fen*	藕粉
Artichokes	*pai ho*	百合
„ Jerusalem	*yü t'ou*	芋頭
Asparagus	*lung hsü t'sai*	龍鬚菜
Bacon	*hsün hsien chu jou*	燻鹹猪肉
Baking powder	*ch'i tzu*	起子
Bamboo shoot	*chu sun*	竹笋
Banana	*hsiang chiao*	香蕉
Barley	*ta mai*	大麥
„ syrup	*mai ya t'ang hsi*	麥芽糖稀
Bay leaf	*hsiang yeh*	香葉
Bean	*tou*	豆
Bean, black	*hei tou*	黑豆

Bean-curd	*tou fu*	豆	腐
Bean flour	*tou fen*	豆	粉
Bean, Lima	*tsan tou*	蠶	豆
Bean, red	*hung tou*	紅	豆
Bean, spaghetti	*tou fen ssu*	豆 粉	絲
Bean-sprouts	*tou ya t'sai*	豆 芽	菜
Bean starch	*tou fen*	豆	粉
Bean, String-	*pien tou*	扁	豆
Bean, white	*pai tou*	白	豆
Beef	*niu jou*	牛	肉
,, brains	*niu nao*	牛	腦
,, Corned	*hsien niu jou*	鹹 牛	肉
,, fillet	*niu li chi*	牛 里	肌
,, heart	*niu hsin*	牛	心
,, kidney	*niu yao*	牛	腰
,, liver	*niu kan*	牛	肝
,, Oxtail	*niu wei*	牛	尾
,, roast	*k'ao cheng k'uai niu jou*	整 塊 牛	肉
,, salt	*hsien niu jou*	鹹 牛	肉
,, shoulder	*niu po ling*	牛 脖	頜
,, soup	*niu jou t'ang*	牛 肉	湯
,, tea	*niu jou ch'ing t'ang*	牛 肉 清	湯
,, tongue	*niu shê*	牛	舌
Beet	*hung t'sai t'ou*	紅 菜	頭
,, -root	*hung t'sai t'ou*	紅 菜	頭
Brain	*nao*		腦

Bran	*fu tzu*	麩子
Bread	*mien pao*	麵包
,, crumbs	*mien pao hsieh*	麵包屑
,, Dry	*kan mien pao*	干麵包
Brussels sprouts	*yang pai t'sai ya*	洋白菜芽
Buckwheat	*ch'ao mai*	蕎麥
,, flour	*ch'ao mai mien*	蕎麥麵
Bustard	*ti pu*	地補油
Butter	*huang yu*	黃油
Cabbage	*pai t'sai*	白菜
,, Chinese	*chung kuo pai t'sai*	中國白菜
,, Foreign	*yang pai t'sai*	洋白菜
,, Red	*hung yang pai t'sai*	紅洋白菜
Cake	*yang kao*	洋糕
Capon	*yen chi*	酪鷄
Carrot	*hu lo po*	胡蘿蔔
Catsup	*hsi hung shih chih*	西紅柿汁
Cauliflower	*pai t'sai hua*	白菜花
Cayenne pepper	*hung ch'uan chiao*	紅川椒
Celery	*ch'in t'sai*	芹菜
,, seed	*ch'in t'sai tzu*	芹菜子
Cheese	*nai yu ping tzu*	奶油餅子
Cherry	*ying t'ao*	櫻桃
Chestnut	*li tzu*	栗子
Chicken	*chi*	鷄
,, fat	*chi yu*	鷄油

Chicken giblet	*chi tsa*	鷄雜肝
„ gizzard	*chi chen kan*	鷄胗肝
„ liver	*chi kan*	鷄肝
„ Smoked	*hsün chi*	燻鷄
Chocolate	*ch'a ke la*	茶格拉
Chutney	*mang kuo chiang*	芒果醬
Cinnamon	*jou kuei*	肉桂
„ Ground	*jou kuei fen*	肉桂粉
„ Stick	*cheng jou kuei*	整肉桂
Citron	*fo shou*	佛手
Clam	*ke li*	蛤蜊
Clove	*ting hsiang*	丁香
„ Ground	*ting hsiang fen*	丁香粉
„ Whole	*cheng ting hsiang*	整丁香
Cocoa	*k'o k'o fen*	蔻蔻粉
Coconut	*hsien yeh tzu*	鮮椰子
Coffee	*ka fei*	咖啡
Corn	*lao yü mi*	老玉米
„ meal	*yü mi mien*	玉米麵
Cornstarch	*yü shu fen*	玉黍粉
Corned beef	*hsien niu jou*	鹹牛肉
Cowpea	*t'san tou*	蠶豆
Crab	*p'ang hsieh*	螃蟹
Crab apple	*hua hung*	花紅
Cracker	*ping kan*	餅乾
Cream	*nai yu*	奶油

Cream, sour	suan nai yu	酸奶油
Cress, Water-	chiao pai	茭白
Cucumber	huang kua	黃瓜
Curd, bean-	tou fu	豆腐
Curry	ka li	蛤唎
„ powder	ka li fen	蛤唎粉
Dates	tsao erh	棗兒
„ Chinese	tsao erh	棗兒
„ Dried	kan tsao erh	干棗兒
„ Honey	mi tsao	蜜棗
„ Red	hung tsao erh	紅棗兒
Dill pickle	suan huang kua	酸黃瓜
Dove	ke tzu	鴿子
Duck, domestic	ya	鴨
„ gizzard	ya chen kan	鴨肫肝
„ liver	ya kan	鴨肝
„ Wild	yeh ya	野鴨
Eel	shan yü	鱔魚
Eggs	tan	蛋
„ Chicken	chi tan	鷄蛋
„ Duck	ya tan	鴨蛋
„ Fish	yü tan	魚蛋
„ Pigeon	ke tan	鴿蛋
„ Smoked	hsün chi tan	燻鷄蛋
„ Tea with	ch'a tan	茶蛋
„ White of	tan pai	蛋白

Egg yolk	*tan huang*	蛋黃
Eggplant	*ch'ieh tzu*	茄子
Endive	*hua yeh sheng t'sai*	花葉生菜
Fig	*wu hua kuo*	無花菓
„ Dried	*kan wu hua kuo*	乾無花菓
Fish	*yü*	魚
„ bass (river)	*ho lu yü*	河鱸魚
„ bass (sea)	*hai lu yu*	海鱸魚
„ bêche-de-mer	*hai shen*	海參
„ bream	*pien yü*	扁魚
„ bream, sea	*ta t'ou yü*	大頭魚
„ bullhead	*ta t'ou yü*	大頭魚
„ carp	*li yü*	鯉魚
„ caviar	*yü tan*	魚蛋
„ clam	*ke li*	蛤蜊
„ cockle	*ke li*	蛤蜊
„ cod	*lu yü*	魯魚
Fish crab	*p'ang hsieh*	螃蟹
„ Dried	*kan yü*	乾魚
„ eel	*shan yü*	鱔魚
„ Globe	*ho t'un yü*	河豚魚
„ herring	*pai yü*	白魚
„ huang chuan	*huang chuan yü*	黃攘魚
„ knife	*tao yü*	刀魚
„ lamprey	*huang shan yü*	黃鱔魚
„ lobster	*lung hsia*	龍蝦

Fish	mackerel	*pa yü*	霸魚
,,	mandarin	*li hua yü*	李花魚
,,	minnow	*hsiao huang kua yü*	小黃瓜魚
,,	mullet	*huang hua yü*	黃花魚
,,	oyster	*hai li tzu*	海蠣子
,,	perch	*kuei yü*	桂魚
,,	perch (sea)	*hai kuei yü*	海桂魚
,,	pike	*yang sha yü*	洋沙魚
,,	plaice	*pi mu yü*	比目魚
,,	prawn	*ta hsia*	大蝦
,,	ray	*yang yü*	洋魚
,,	roach	*fu yü*	福魚
,,	salmon	*sha men yü*	沙門魚
,,	sea-slugs	*hai shen*	海參
,,	shark fin	*yü ch'ih*	魚翅
,,	shrimps	*hsia mi*	蝦米
,,	shuttle	*lêng yü*	棱魚
,,	Smoked	*hsün yü*	燻魚
,,	sole	*chien yü*	尖魚
,,	sturgeon	*hui wang yü*	惠王魚
,,	tunny	*t'ai pa yü*	抬壩魚
,,	turbot	*p'ing tzu yü*	瓶子魚
,,	whitebait	*yin yü*	銀魚
Flour		*pai mien*	白麵
,,	Bean	*tou mien*	豆麵
,,	Buckwheat	*ch'ao mai mien*	蕎麥麵

Flour, grain whole wheat	*ch'uan mai mien*	全	麥	麵
,, Millet	*hsiao mi mien*	小米		麵
,, Rice	*mi fên mien*	米粉		麵
,, Wheat	*pai mien*	白		麵
Frog (edible)	*t'ien chi*	田		鷄
Fungus	*mu erh*	木		耳
Garlic	*suan*			蒜
Gelatine	*tung wu chiao*	動 物		膠
Gherkin	*hsiao huang kua*	小黃		瓜
Giblet	*chi tsa*	鷄		雜
Ginger	*chiang*			薑
,, Candied	*t'ang sheng chiang*	糖 生		薑
,, Preserved	*t'ang chiang*	糖		薑
,, Powdered	*chiang fen*	薑		粉
,, Root	*chiang*			薑
Goose	*o*			鵝
,, Domestic	*chia o*	家		鵝
,, Wild	*yeh o*	野		鵝
Gooseberry	*ying yu kuo*	嬰 薁		果
Grape	*p'u t'ao*	葡		萄
,, Red	*hung p'u t'ao*	紅 葡		萄
,, White	*pai p'u t'ao*	白 葡		萄
Grapefruit	*mei kuo yu tzu*	美 國		柚子
Grouse	*shih chi*	食		鷄
,, Sand-	*sha chi*	沙		鷄
Ham	*huo t'ui*	火		腿

Hare	*yeh mao*	野貓
Honey	*feng mi*	蜂蜜
Horse-radish	*la ken*	辣根
Horse-radish (prepared)	*la ken ni tzu*	辣根泥子
Hops	*she ma t'sao*	蛇蔴草
Jam	*t'ang chiang*	糖醬
Jelly	*ch'ing t'ang chiang*	清糖醬
Jujube	*tsao erh*	棗兒
Kale	*yu t'sai*	油菜
Kaoliang	*kao liang*	高糧
Ketchup	*hsi hung shih chih*	西紅柿汁
Kidney	*yao*	腰
Lamb	*hsiao yang jou*	小羊肉
,, Chop	*hsiao yang jou p'ai ku*	小羊肉排骨
,, kidney	*hsiao yang yao*	小羊腰
,, Leg of	*hsiao yang t'ui*	小羊腿
,, liver	*hsiao yang kan*	小羊肝
,, tongue	*hsiao yang she*	小羊舌
Lard	*chu yu*	豬油
Leek	*chiu t'sai*	韭菜
,, sprout (chou t'sai)	*hsiao chiu t'sai*	小韭菜
Lemon	*hsiang t'ao*	香桃兒
,, Chinese	*hsiang yuan*	香橼
,, Foreign	*yang hsiang t'ao*	洋香桃
,, juice	*hsiang t'ao chih*	香桃汁
,, peel	*hsiang t'ao p'i*	香桃皮

Lentil		pan tou	半豆菜梅
Lettuce		sheng t'sai	生菜梅
Lime		ch'ing mei	青梅
Litchi		li chih	荔枝
,,	Dried	kan li chih	乾荔枝
Liver		kan	肝
,,	Beef	niu kan	牛肝
,,	Calf	hsiao niu kan	小牛肝
,,	Chicken	chi kan	鷄肝
,,	Duck	ya kan	鴨肝
,,	Goose	o kan	鵝肝
,,	Pig	chu kan	猪肝
,,	Sheep	yang kan	羊肝
Lotus		lien hua	蓮花
,,	root	ou	藕
,,	seeds	lien hua tzu	蓮花子
,,	starch	ou fen	藕粉
Mace		hui hsiang	茴香
Mango		mang kuo	芒菓
Marrow		tung kua	冬瓜
Melon		kua	瓜
,,	Cantaloup	t'ien kua	甜瓜
,,	Water	hsi kua	西瓜
Milk		nai	奶
,,	Cow's	niu nai	牛奶
,,	Goat's	shan yang nai	山羊奶

Milk, powdered	*nai fen*		奶粉
,, Preserved	*kuan t'ou niu nai*	罐頭牛奶	
,, Sour	*suan nai*		酸奶
Millet	*hsiao mi*		小米
Mint	*po ho*		薄荷
Molasses	*hung t'ang hsi*	紅糖稀	
Mushroom	*mo ko*		蘑菇
,, Button	*k'ou mo*		口蘑
,, Dried	*kan k'ou mo*	乾口蘑	
Mustard	*chieh mo*		芥末
,, -seed	*chieh mo tzu*	芥末子	
Mutton	*yang jou*		羊肉
,, brains	*yang nao*		羊腦
,, chop	*yang p'ai ku*	羊排骨	
,, fat	*yang yu*		羊油
,, heart	*yang hsin*		羊心
Mutton	*yang jou*		羊肉
,, Leg of	*yang t'ui*		羊腿
,, kidney	*yang yao*		羊腰
,, liver	*yang kan*		羊肝
,, shoulder	*yang po ling*	羊脖領	
,, tongue	*yang she*		羊舌
Noodles	*mien t'iao*		麵條
Nutmeg	*tou k'ou*		豆寇
Oil	*yu*		油
,, Bean	*tou yu*		豆油

Oil castor	*ta ma yu*	大蓖油
„ Peanut	*hua sheng yu*	花生油
„ Sesame	*ma yu*	蓖油
„ Tea	*ch'a yu*	茶油
„ Vegetable seed	*t'sai yu*	菜油
Okra	*yang chi chiao*	羊犄角
Olive	*ch'ing kuo*	青菓
Olive oil	*ch'ing kuo yu*	青菓油
Onion	*ts'ung t'ou*	葱頭
„ Spring	*ch'ing suan*	青蒜
Orange	*chü tzu*	橘子
„ Canton	*kuang chü*	廣橘
„ Golden	*chin chü*	金橘
„ Honey	*mi chü*	蜜橘
„ Tangerine	*mi kan*	蜜干
Parsley	*hsiang t'sai*	香菜
Parsnip	*pa chiao*	芭蕉
Partridge	*an ch'un*	鵪鶉
Pea	*wan tou*	莞豆
„ Cow-	*ts'an tou*	蠶豆
„ Dried	*kan tou*	乾豆
„ Green	*lü wan tou*	綠莞豆
Peach	*t'ao erh*	桃兒
Peanut	*hua sheng*	花生子
Pear	*li tzu*	蔾
Pepper	*hu chiao*	胡椒

Pepper cayenne	*hung ch'uan chiao*	紅川椒
„ Corns	*hu chiao tzu*	胡椒子
„ Green	*ch'ing la chiao*	青辣椒
„ Ground	*hu chiao mien*	胡椒麵
„ Red	*hung la chiao*	紅辣椒
Persimmon	*shih tzu*	柿子
„ Dried	*kan shih tzu*	乾柿子
Pheasant	*yeh chi*	野鷄
Pickle	*chiang t'sai*	醬菜
Pineapple	*po lo kuo*	菠蘿菓
Pine-nut	*sung tzu*	松子
Pigeon	*ke tzu*	鴿子
„ Wild	*yeh ke tzu*	野鴿子
Pistachio	*fei tzu*	榧子
Plover	*shui chi tzu*	水鷄子
Plum	*li tzu*	李子
Pomelo	*yu tzu*	柚子
Pomegranate	*shih liu*	石榴
Pork	*chu jou*	猪肉
„ brain	*chu nao*	猪腦
„ breast	*chu p'ai ku*	猪排骨
„ feet, pigs	*chu t'i*	猪蹄
„ fillet	*chu li chi*	猪里肌
„ heart	*chu hsin*	猪心
„ kidney	*chu yao*	猪腰
„ leg	*chu t'ui*	猪腿

Pork liver	*chu kan*	猪肝
Pork, salted	*hsien chu jou*	鹹猪肉
Potato	*shan yao tou*	山藥豆
„ Sweet	*pai shu*	白薯
Preserves	*t'ang chiang*	糖醬
Prune	*yang wu mei*	洋烏梅
„ Black	*hei tsao erh*	黑棗兒
Pumpkin	*wo kua*	倭瓜
Quail	*an ch'un*	鵪鶉
Quince	*mu kua*	木瓜
Rabbit	*yeh mao*	野貓
Radish	*hsiao hung lo po*	小紅蘿蔔
Raisin	*p'u t'ao kan*	葡萄乾
„ Black	*hei p'u t'ao kan*	黑葡萄乾
„ White	*pai p'u t'ao kan*	白葡萄乾
Red haws	*shan ch'a*	山查
Rhubarb	*ta huang*	大黃
Rice	*mi*	米
„ flour	*mi mien*	米麵
„ Glutinous	*no mi*	糯米
„ Korean	*kao li mi*	高麗米
„ Popped	*ch'ao mi*	炒米
„ spaghetti	*mi fen ssu*	米粉絲
Sage	*tzu su*	紫蘇
Salsify	*pai ken t'sai*	白根菜
Salt	*hsien yen*	鹹鹽

Sausage	*ch'ang tzu*	腸子	
„ Meat	*ch'ang tzu sui jou*	腸子碎肉	
„ Pork	*chu jou ch'ang tzu*	猪肉腸子	
„ Smoked	*hsün chang tzu*	燻腸子	
Sea blubber	*hai che*	海蜇	
Seaweed	*hai tai t'sai*	海岱菜	
Sesame	*chih ma*	芝蔴	
„ oil	*chih ma yu*	芝蔴油	
„ seed	*chih ma tzu*	芝蔴子	
Shrimp	*hsia mi*	蝦米	
„ Dried	*kan hsia jen*	乾蝦仁	
Snipe	*shui cha*	水扎	
Soda	*chien*	鹼	
Sorrel	*suan yeh*	酸葉	
Sauerkraut	*yen pai t'sai*	醃白菜	
Soya sauce	*chiang yu*	醬油	
Spinach	*po t'sai*	菠菜	
Squash	*nan kua*	南瓜	
Steak	*jou p'ai*	肉排	
„ Beef	*niu jou p'ai*	牛肉排	
„ Veal	*hsiao niu jou p'ai*	小牛肉排	
Strawberry	*yang mei*	洋梅	
Suet	*niu yu*	牛油	
Sugar	*t'ang*	糖	
„ Brown	*hung t'ang*	紅糖	

Sugar lump	*k'uai t'ang*	塊糖	
,, Powdered	*hsi pai t'ang fen*	細白糖粉	
,, Rock	*ping t'ang*	冰糖	
,, White	*pai t'ang*	白糖	
Sweetbread	*niu i tzu*	牛膵子	
Syrup	*t'ang hsi*	糖稀	
,, Barley	*mai ya t'ang hsi*	麥芽糖稀	
,, Malt	*mai ya t'ang hsi*	麥芽糖稀	
Tea	*ch'a*	茶	
,, Beef-	*niu jou ch'ing t'ang*	牛肉清湯	
,, Chinese	*chung kuo ch'a yeh*	中國茶葉	
Tea, green	*lu ch'a*	綠茶	
,, Red	*hung ch'a*	紅茶	
Teal	*hsiao shui ya*	小水鴨	
Tomato	*hsi hung shih*	西紅柿	
,, catsup	*hsi hung shih chih*	西紅柿汁	
,, Green	*ch'ing hsi hung shih*	青西紅柿	
,, juice	*hsi hung shih shui*	西紅柿水	
,, puree	*hsi hung shih ni tzu*	西紅柿泥子	
,, sauce	*hsi hung shih t'ang*	西紅柿湯	
Tongue	*she*	舌	
,, Beef	*niu she*	牛舌	
,, Lamb	*hsiao yang she*	小羊舌	
,, Mutton	*yang she*	羊舌	
,, Pig	*chu she*	猪舌	

Tongue smoked	*hsün niu she*	燻牛舌	
Turkey	*hoa chi*	火鷄	
Turnip	*lo po*	蘿蔔	
Vanilla	*hsiang chao chih*	香蕉汁	
Veal	*hsiao niu jou*	小牛肉	
„ chop	*hsiao niu jou p'ai ku*	小牛肉排骨	
„ liver	*hsiao niu jou kan*	小牛肉肝	
„ steak	*hsiao nio jou p'ai*	小牛肉排	
Venison	*lu jou*	鹿肉	
Vinegar	*t'su*	醋	
„ Chinese	*mi t'su*	米醋	
„ Foreign	*yang t'su*	洋醋	
Walnut	*ho t'ao*	核桃	
Water-chestnut	*pi ch'i*	荸薺	
Watercress	*chiao pai*	茭白	
Water-melon	*hsi kua*	西瓜	
Wine, Chinese	*huang chiu*	黃酒	
Yeast	*fa mien fen*	發麵粉	

*Some other Oxford Paperbacks for readers
interested in Central Asia, China and
South-east Asia, past and present*

CAMBODIA

GEORGE COEDÈS
Angkor: An Introduction

CENTRAL ASIA

PETER FLEMING
Bayonets to Lhasa

LADY MACARTNEY
An English Lady in
Chinese Turkestan

ALBERT VON LE COQ
Buried Treasures of
Chinese Turkestan

AITCHEN WU
Turkistan Tumult

CHINA

HAROLD ACTON
Peonies and Ponies

PETER FLEMING
The Siege at Peking

W. SOMERSET MAUGHAM
On a Chinese Screen

G. E. MORRISON
An Australian in China

OSBERT SITWELL
Escape with Me! An
Oriental Sketch-book

INDONESIA

S. TAKDIR ALISJAHBANA
Indonesia: Social and
Cultural Revolution

DAVID ATTENBOROUGH
Zoo Quest for a Dragon

VICKI BAUM
A Tale from Bali

MIGUEL COVARRUBIAS
Island of Bali

JACQUES DUMARCAY
Borobudur

JENNIFER LINDSAY
Javanese Gamelan

EDWIN M. LOEB
Sumatra: Its History and
People

MOCHTAR LUBIS
Twilight in Djakarta

MADELON H. LULOFS
Coolie

ANNA MATHEWS
The Night of Purnama

COLIN McPHEE
A House in Bali

HICKMAN POWELL
The Last Paradise

BERYL DE ZOETE AND
WALTER SPIES
Dance and Drama in
Bali

E. R. SCIDMORE
Java, Garden of the East

LADISLAO SZÉKELY
Tropic Fever: The
Adventures of a Planter
in Sumatra

EDWARD C. VAN NESS
AND
SHITA PRAWIROHARDJO
Javanese Wayang Kulit

AUGUSTA DE WIT
Java: Facts and Fancies

MALAYSIA

ABDULLAH ABDUL KADIR
The Hikayat Abdullah

ISABELLA L. BIRD
The Golden Chersonese:
Travels in Malaya in
1879

PIERRE BOULLE
Sacrilege in Malaya.

C. C. BROWN (Editor)
Sejarah Melayu or Malay
Annals

COLIN N. CRISSWELL
Rajah Charles Brooke:
Monarch of All He
Surveyed

C. T. DOBREE
Gambling Games of
Malaya

K. M. ENDICOTT
An Analysis of Malay
Magic

HENRI FAUCONNIER
The Soul of Malaya

JOHN D. GIMLETTE
Malay Poisons and
Charm Cures

JOHN D. GIMLETTE AND
H. W. THOMSON
A Dictionary of Malayan
Medicine

A. G. GLENISTER
The Birds of the Malay
Peninsula, Singapore
and Penang

C. W. HARRISON
Illustrated Guide to the
Federated Malay States
(1923)

TOM HARRISSON
World Within

DENNIS HOLMAN
Noone of the Ulu

CHARLES HOSE
The Field-Book of a
Jungle Wallah

SYBIL KATHIGASU
No Dram of Mercy

MALCOLM MacDONALD
Borneo People

W. SOMERSET MAUGHAM
The Casuarina Tree

MARY McMINNIES
The Flying Fox

AMBROSE B. RATHBORNE
Camping and Tramping
  in Malaya

ROBERT W. C. SHELFORD
A Naturalist in Borneo

J. T. THOMSON
Glimpses into Life in
  Malayan Lands

RICHARD WINSTEDT
The Malay Magician

PHILIPPINES

AUSTIN COATES
Rizal

SINGAPORE

PATRICK ANDERSON
Snake Wine: A Singapore
  Episode

ROLAND BRADDELL
The Lights of Singapore

R. W. E. HARPER AND
HARRY MILLER
Singapore Mutiny

JANET LIM
Sold for Silver

G. M. REITH
Handbook to Singapore
  (1907)

C. E. WURTZBURG
Raffles of the Eastern Isles

THAILAND

REGINALD CAMPBELL
Teak Wallah

ERIK SEIDENFADEN
Guide to Bangkok (1928)

MALCOLM SMITH
A Physician at the Court
  of Siam

ERNEST YOUNG
The Kingdom of the
  Yellow Robe